Heart
Of A
Handmaiden

by Cathy Corle

Revival Fires! Publishing
P.O. Box 245
Claysburg, PA 16625
814/239-2813

Table of Contents

To My Dear Sister In Christ,

I don't know when I've ever been as excited about getting a book into someone's hands as I am about this one. I guess it's because the messages here are the most personal and most needed ones in my own life.

Some of the things printed in these pages are the things the Holy Spirit has whispered in my heart at those crucial 'crossroads' moments in my life. Some of the sweetest and most encouraging truths have illuminated the dark valleys and others have motivated and invigorated me for the steep, upward climbs. There are principles and promises that have helped me to 'keep on keeping on,' that I plan to turn to again when I need them. I hope that putting them in print here will cause someone else to keep on, as well.

Isaiah was a servant of God in the midst of a time of judgment and peril. He was called upon to give God's message to his beloved nation, God's chosen people who had turned their backs upon His word and His will. Perhaps we have something in common with Isaiah and others like him who God used in such times in history. No doubt, we're living in such days right now.

In the sixth chapter, we see Isaiah as he gets a good look at the <u>awesomeness</u> of <u>a</u> holy <u>God</u>. *"In the year that king Uzziah died I saw also the Lord sitting upon a throne, high and lifted up, and his train filled the temple. Above it stood the seraphims: each one had six wings; with twain he covered his face, and with twain he covered his feet, and with twain he did fly. And one cried unto another, and said, Holy, holy, holy, is the Lord of hosts: the whole earth is full of his glory. And the posts of the door moved at the voice of him that cried, and the house was filled with smoke."*

A clear view of God's holiness caused him to be stricken with the <u>awfulness</u> of <u>his</u> <u>sinful</u> <u>self</u>. *"Then said I,*

Woe is me! for I am undone; because I am a man of unclean lips, and I dwell in the midst of a people of unclean lips: for mine eyes have seen the King, the Lord of hosts." Getting your eyes on the Lord doesn't automatically make you feel worthy or capable of being a servant of God; on the contrary, it makes us acutely aware of our own unworthiness and inabilities. But it leads us to the next step.

Once he confessed his own uncleanness, then cleansing was available. *"Then flew one of the seraphims unto me, having a live coal in his hand, which he had taken with the tongs from off the altar: And he laid it upon my mouth, and said, Lo, this hath touched thy lips; and thine iniquity is taken away, and thy sin purged."* Cleanness is a prerequisite to usefulness.

Once he had a clear view of God and a good look at himself, and he made contact with the cleansing power of God, then God called on him to serve. *"Also I heard the voice of the Lord, saying, Whom shall I send, and who will go for us? Then said I, Here am I; send me."*

I don't know about you, but I have to be reminded over and over again that I'm not the first person to be painfully aware of my own unworthiness and inability to be of any use to the Lord. It's always a fresh, happy, surprising re-discovery for me that God's all-sufficiency is available to replace my insufficiency. He didn't ask me to be great, just to proclaim His greatness. I don't need any special powers; I just need to be a pipeline for His power. I don't need to be anything but available. I don't need to do anything but volunteer.

When self is surrendered to the Savior, and my insufficiency is swallowed up in His all-sufficiency, then the miraculous can take place, and God can do His life-changing work -- even through me.

"Behold the
handmaid of
the Lord;
be it unto me
according to
thy word..."
Luke 1:38

This book is lovingly and prayerfully dedicated to
every lady who gives her heart and life to be the
Lord's handmaiden, and most especially to
many dear friends who are preachers' wives.
The Lord has abundantly blessed me through the
years with the opportunity to know some of the
sweetest and most faithful ladies in the world.
It is my hope that what is written in these pages will
both uplift your soul and mirror your heart's desire.

The Preacher's Wife

There's a lady in most every church
Who gives God all her life;
Each day she lives in serving Him,
She is the Preacher's Wife.
There are very few who see the heart
Beyond the smiling face,
Her burdens and the work she does --
No one could take her place.

5

Heart of a Handmaiden

Her ministries are many,
Sometime washing dirty clothes,
Wiping dishes, spills, and tears,
Or the baby's nose.
A kind word of love or comfort,
Or some steaming dish of food,
Sharing tears and laughter,
And speaking just the good.

She might sing or play piano,
Or teach in Sunday School,
She may type the Preacher's letters,
And make sure his coffee's full.
There are many jobs she sees to
That the members could have done,
There are many nights she's weary
At the setting of the sun.

But where she specializes
Is the man who is her life;
Her first responsibility,
For she's the Preacher's Wife.
She prays him through the worst times,
And she cheers him through the best,
She does things the way he likes them,
And fills his each request.

Heart of a Handmaiden

She tells him all his sermons
Are the best she's ever heard
And she's proud that he is faithful
In the preaching of God's Word.
She assures him that his coat and tie
Are the world's most perfect match,
She tells him that he's handsome
And she's glad that he's attached.

She carries all his children
'Neath her heart, then in her arms;
She nurses them through illness
And checks that they are warm.
She teaches them of Jesus' love
And leads them to the Lord,
She teaches them to say,
"We've got he best Daddy in the world!"

She lives life in a hurry,
Sometimes without life's finer things,
But without one time complaining
She accepts what praying brings.
There's a time of great rewarding
When we reach the end of life,
And only then the world will know
The greatness of the Preacher's Wife.

by Cathy Corle

"Even so must
their wives
be grave,
not slanderers,
sober, faithful
in all things."
I Timothy 3:11

Chapter One

Unlikely Choices

"For ye see your calling, brethren, how that not many wise men after the flesh, not many mighty, not many noble, are called: But God hath chosen the foolish things of the world to confound the wise; and God hath chosen the weak things of the world to confound the things which are mighty; And base things of the world, and things which are despised, hath God chosen, yea, and things which are not, to bring to nought things that are: That no flesh should glory in his presence...That your faith should not stand in the wisdom of men, but in the power of God." (I Corinthians 1:26-29; 2:5)

Have you ever wondered why God chooses to use the people that He uses greatly? As a young girl and even as a young preacher's wife, it seemed very easy for me to see why God would use a John Rice or a Lee Roberson or a Tom Malone. Why, because they're such great and godly individuals, of course! But in light of what I saw in them, why and how would God ever use someone like plain old, everyday me?

What I didn't realize was that I was looking at the finished product, and not the raw materials. I was admiring the lives of people whom God had blessed and empowered and used in a great way for many years, and seeing what their lives had become. But I was not seeing what that life had been when it was placed in God's hand many years prior. Thus, even though there was a desire in the hidden depths of my heart, I had very little confidence that God could do much with me, and I really wasn't sure He would even want to.

At a conference a few years ago, I conveyed my amazement to a friend. Here was Dr. Malone and Dr. Hyles, and then here I was in the middle of it as a speaker's wife and a soloist. I said, "Maybe this is how it would feel if a Little League short stop wandered out into the playing field during the World Series! What am I doing here, anyway? I'm just a nobody!"

In spite of my lack of faith, I've seen God do some miraculous things through our lives and ministry through the years. When my husband and I married, we talked excitedly and made plans about how we would love to hold revival meetings and see people saved and be used of God together. It seemed to me like too much to ask, but we've truly seen God do 'exceedingly abundantly above all that we asked or thought.' Yet, I don't think I ever got away from the feeling of insufficiency that I started out with. Maybe you'll understand why this lesson from the Lord was such an exciting one for me.

"And Elijah the Tishbite, who was of the inhabitants of Gilead, said unto Ahab, As the LORD God of Israel liveth, before whom I stand, there shall not be dew nor rain these years, but according to my word. And the word of the LORD came unto him, saying, Get thee hence, and

turn thee eastward, and hide thyself by the brook Cherith, that is before Jordan. And it shall be, that thou shalt drink of the brook; and I have commanded the ravens to feed thee there. So he went and did according unto the word of the LORD: for he went and dwelt by the brook Cherith, that is before Jordan. And the ravens brought him bread and flesh in the morning, and bread and flesh in the evening; and he drank of the brook.."

"And it came to pass after a while, that the brook dried up, because there had been no rain in the land. And the word of the LORD came unto him, saying, Arise, get thee to Zarephath, which belongeth to Zidon, and dwell there: behold, I have commanded a widow woman there to sustain thee. So he arose and went to Zarephath. And when he came to the gate of the city, behold, the widow woman was there gathering of sticks: and he called to her, and said, Fetch me, I pray thee, a little water in a vessel, that I may drink. And as she was going to fetch it, he called to her, and said, Bring me, I pray thee, a morsel of bread in thine hand. And she said, As the LORD thy God liveth, I have not a cake, but an handful of meal in a barrel, and a little oil in a cruse: and behold, I am gathering two sticks, that I may go in and dress it for me and my son, that we may eat it, and die."

"And Elijah said unto her, Fear not; go and do as thou hast said: but make me thereof a little cake first, and bring it unto me, and after make for thee and for thy son. For thus saith the LORD God of Israel, The barrel of meal shall not waste, neither shall the cruse of oil fail, until the day that the LORD sendeth rain upon the earth. And she went and did according to the saying of Elijah: and she, and he, and her house, did eat many days. And the barrel of meal wasted not, neither did the cruse of oil fail, according to the word of the LORD, which he spake by Elijah." (I Kings

11

17:1-16)

The thing that stood out to me first from this story was that God gave this woman a job to do that was seemingly impossible. My first thought was rather humorous. "Well, if I was going to pick someone out to feed the man of God for a year and a half, I would have looked for someone with plenty of food!"

If it were my job to determine who was qualified for this job, I probably would have looked for a farm where the barns were overflowing and the gardens were brimming over with lots of yummy produce. If I couldn't have found that, I would have looked for who had the most food and the least mouths to feed. But not the Lord! That would be too easy. That would seem very natural, when God gets glory from the supernatural. That would look like the individual really did something of merit, when God gets glory from situations where He has to do it or nothing will get done.

I think that God must love the word 'impossible.' It's always seemed to be a discouraging word to me, and I'm only just beginning to realize how God wants me to look at those situations and jobs and needs that are labeled 'impossible.' Here we have a situation where God has decided to meet the need in the life of His prophet, and since He loves dealing with the impossible, the woman that God chose to feed Elijah was a woman who had almost no food.

I thought, "Lord, I may not be able to identify with all these great and noble people who serve You, but I think I can identify with this lady. She was totally incapable of doing the job You wanted her to do, and that's exactly how I feel. So maybe, in rare cases, God does choose to use someone who is completely unqualified. In that case, God might use me, too." In my pondering, I thought, "This must be a special case. God wouldn't use her if He could find

12

someone better suited to the task." But the Holy Spirit wasn't finished with me yet. The Lord reminded me of several things.

When God's plan was for a great prophet or important leader to be born, and even the Savior of the world, who did He choose? While I would have looked for someone who had plenty of experience with motherhood, God often chose a woman who was barren, and completely unable to have a child.

When God wanted to use a woman to give history's greatest lesson in sacrificial giving, you would expect Him to look for someone with a lot of money, right? Wrong again. He chose the woman with only two mites, who was willing to give it all.

When God was going to give us the one documented story in history where one lady soulwinner was used to turn an entire city upside down with the gospel, and to reach great numbers of people in one day, who did He choose? The lady who really knew a lot about the Bible? The woman who had plenty of training and experience and methods in soulwinning? The woman with the spotless reputation and sterling character who was respected by all?

No, God used the little Samaritan woman who had been married five times and was currently living in adultery. She had no tracts, no New Testament, no memorized verses or outlined plan of salvation. All she had was the testimony of what Christ had done for her, and the new-born glow of joy and forgiveness and excitement about God's love and mercy to her.

When God was going to give an outline of the character of the godly, virtuous woman, who did He use? Out of all the women in history He could have chosen, who was the woman that was instrumental in the writing of Proverbs 31? Well, think with me for a moment... who wrote the book of

Proverbs? It was Solomon. King Solomon, being a man, had to learn what God desired and expected in a woman from someone else, and verse one of that chapter tells who it was. *"The words of King Lemuel, the prophecy that his mother taught him."* Now, who was the king's mother? It was Bathsheba who, in the minds of people, will always be synonymous with an adulterous affair, but who found forgiveness and cleansing in the eyes of God. When God chose to teach virtue and godliness to all the women in history, He used someone who had lost her own virtue, and then placed herself under the purifying blood of the Redeemer.

Do you ever wonder about God's sense of humor? God stumped all the Pharisees by using people in His service that they wouldn't have used to feed their dog. Remember the attitude of the Pharisees when Christ ate with publicans and sinners, and when he allowed a forgiven harlot to wash His feet with her tears?

The Pharisees are still with us today. There are a great number of folks who might not do much for God themselves, but they feel appointed to determine who is qualified to serve God, and who is unqualified. "If you've got this sin or that sin in your past, you could never be forgiven and cleansed and justified. God could never use you. You're all washed up." According to their doctrine, there are some sins that can be washed away, and then there are other sins that will stain your record eternally, regardless of the blood of Christ.

But people are sinners, and God uses people. God doesn't ask the Pharisees for their permission before He uses them, either. There's no one that is beyond God's power to cleanse and forgive and transform. *"Know ye not that the unrighteous shall not inherit the kingdom of God? Be not deceived: neither fornicators, nor idolaters, nor adulterers, nor effeminate, nor abusers of themselves with mankind, Nor thieves, nor covetous, nor drunkards, nor revilers, nor extortioners, shall inherit the kingdom of God. And such WERE some of you: but ye are washed, but ye are sanctified, but ye are justified in the name of the Lord Jesus, and by the Spirit of our God." (I Corinthians 6:9-11)*

Maybe the critics have never read enough Bible to realize that the three men God used to pen most of the Bible were all three murderers --- Moses, David, and Paul. They missed the fact that some of the women who were most involved in Jesus' life and ministry were converted harlots.

When God wrote the Bible, He didn't extol all the virtues of people like we tend to do, and cover up their backslidings and failures. Neither did He tell all the ugly details, and fail to mention that they tried to serve God, and they followed God and prayed and were used to accomplish great things for His glory at other times. God just told us all of it. I think He wanted us to realize that He doesn't use just a few choice people who have been sinlessly perfect from the day they were born, and the rest of us are doomed to a life of meaningless existence. God wanted us to see that He saves and cleanses and transforms and USES real people, just like you and me.

I began by thinking that this widow in Zaraphath was the most unqualified person God could have chosen, but after examining these facts, I think I understand. God chooses to use the weak, the foolish, the seemingly unqualified and incapable, so that the world will know that God did it. The least qualified is often the most qualified in God's scheme of things. A preacher made this statement and I wrote it down in my Bible. "It is possible to be too big for God to use, but it's never possible to be too little for God to use."

15

In the first part of the chapter, Elijah had to hide from the wicked king while God's judgment was being carried out. God told him exactly where to go, and when he obeyed God's direction, his needs were met. God said to him, *"...I have commanded the ravens to feed thee there."* We've all spent some time in science class talking about animal instincts, and the amazing things that the Creator has instilled in their intelligence about migration and survival. It's no hard task for God to instill in these 'bird-brains' that He wanted them to deliver meals to a man by the brook twice a day. No questions. No argument. No excuses. Those birds did what God commanded them to do. Where did they get the food? I doubt that the ravens had a supply of bread and meat on a regular basis, yet when God commanded these birds, He provided everything that was necessary for them to do the job. Sounds easy so far.

The very judgment that Elijah had pronounced caused the brook to dry up that had sustained him during the first part of his exile. It was time to go on to part two of the plan. Again, God told him exactly where to go, and promised provision when he got there. *"...behold, I have commanded a widow woman there to sustain thee."* God commanded this woman to feed Elijah just like He had commanded the ravens. God didn't say, "I will command her;" He said, "I have commanded her." I believe that she knew within what God wanted her to do just as much as those birds had known. She already felt the direction, the command, the burden, whatever you want to call it. God had already told her. No questions, arguments, or excuses, right?

Elijah walked into town and found the woman there gathering sticks. He said, "Would you get me a drink of water? And while you're at it, would you fix me some supper, too?" Here's her opportunity to be used of God.

16

Here's her chance to obey God's command and do what she already knew God had called on her to do. And she said, "Who, me? I could never do that! I don't have what it takes!"

Now I'm really feeling comfortable with this lady. How many times has God burdened your heart about meeting a need, or getting involved in a ministry, or reaching out to someone, and in your heart you knew God wanted you to do it. Yet, when the opportunity arose, you jumped back with the same response. "Who me? I'm unqualified. I couldn't do something like that. I don't have what it takes. That's impossible." It really was impossible for her to feed the prophet with her own resources, but she hadn't yet learned that "Where God guides, He provides." God's commands are His enablings. If He told her to do the job, He'll give her everything needed to get it done. Though I've had plenty of lessons, sometimes I act like I haven't learned it, either.

Imagine what may have been on her mind. "It's not fair. We're ready to starve, and God wants me to take the little food I have and give it to a total stranger. Doesn't God care about my family?" But she did not know yet that her family's need would be met by God if she would allow the need of God's prophet to be met by her. Their livelihood depended on her willingness to 'trust and obey,' to give her little handful to God and know that He will give back all that is given to Him, and His handfuls are much bigger than ours. She could have kept her little handful that would make one meager meal for herself and her son. They would have eaten it and then died. But instead she gave her little handful to God, and God stretched her resources to meet the need of the prophet, herself, and her entire household for as long as the drought lasted.

An impossibility is simply a platform from which God

can work a miracle. There would be no need for a miracle if we never faced those impossible situations. If we could see our lives from God's viewpoint, those same frustrating circumstances might just be a disguise for exciting opportunities that God will use to do great things for us. But first we have to step out by faith when God calls on us to do the impossible, and obediently give our little handful to God, whatever it is that we have and God wants to use.

You say, "I would like to serve God and do what He's called on me to do, but it's impossible, I told you. How can I do the impossible?" In John 15:5 Jesus said, *"...Without me ye can do nothing."* We already knew that, didn't we? That's what we've been trying to make God understand all along. But further on in the New Testament God gives us the key that unlocks all the possibilities of what God could use us to do for Him. *"I can do all things through Christ which strengtheneth me." (Philippians 4:13)* I can't do the impossible, but the Lord can. If I'm saved, He lives within my heart. He is capable where I am incapable. He is wise and all-powerful where I am foolish and limited. What I cannot do in my own strength, I can do in the strength of Christ who works in me and through me. That means that there is nothing that God leads me to do that I cannot do. He will provide what I lack. Now all my excuses are fading...

Two different college presidents of good Bible colleges have told us the same story. The two or three students in their history who were the most talented, the best preachers, seemed to have the most potential, whom everyone expected to turn the world upside down in short order are the ones who are not even in the ministry today. But they have graduates who are building great churches and being used of God mightily who, when they were college students, the faculty wondered if they could get their shoes on the right feet. Why is that?

God loves to use the 'least likely to succeed,' because then He gets the glory. Not only that, but the person who recognizes his own inability is going to be the most likely to depend upon God's power instead of his own. It seems quite logical that you need God's power to do God's work, yet we've all been guilty of beating our heads against the wall trying to do it on our own. I think that's why often the most timid person becomes the boldest soulwinner. That's why the poorest people often become the most generous givers. That's why often it's the people with the poorest health and least natural ability who become the most active and most valuable people in a church or ministry. When we see our insufficiency, we're ready to draw on God's all-sufficiency.

I once illustrated the same thought like this. When I was looking forward to becoming a mother, I had every intention in the world of being the best. I had learned all the formulas, how-to's, do's and don'ts. I had read the books and listened to the tapes. I knew everything there was to know about how to be the perfect mother until something terrible happened. You're right... I had children. Like everyone embarking on an important mission, I had Plan A tucked under my arm and everything was going smoothly... for five minutes or so. But Plan A died with the plant I brought home from the hospital, so I dusted off my confidence, made a few adjustments, and set out determinedly with Plan B. It didn't take long until Plan B was shattered hopelessly at my feet, and I had to grit my teeth, let out a sigh, and carve out a Plan C. But I knew I could do it.

When I had exhausted all my plans along with all of the alphabet, and Plan Z was now in it's grave, I finally dissolved into tears. "God, I know this is something You want me to do, and I want to do it for You, but I've discovered that I can't. I don't know where to start. Every attempt falls flat on its face. God, I'm willing, I'm just not able. If you want this important job cared for, You're going to have to do it, with me or without me." When I thought I'd come to a dead end, I found a new door open. God said, "It's about time. That's exactly what I've been waiting for."

Now why don't I start out there? Why do I have to face so much frustration and disappointment and defeat before I say, "Lord, I can't do it on my own. You'll have to do it, or it won't get done." I need to realize at the beginning of a task, that if it's God's work, then I can't do it without His help. Without Him I can do nothing, but through Him I can do all things. Someone said, "When you've come to the very end of your strength, you're only at the beginning of God's."

Early in the ministry of D. L. Moody, a business man heard of his Sunday School endeavors among Chicago's poor people, and how God was using him. He was interested to see this for himself, so he inquired about the time and location and was present at the next service. The location turned out to be an abandoned house where he found a few drunkards and uncultured adults and a good many children in dirty, ragged clothing. The man sat near the back of the room and observed as Moody sat down with a Bible and a little child on his lap and began to read about the Prodigal Son. He stumbled through the story, and skipped some words entirely that he was unable to pronounce. But to his amazement, this man saw people weeping and responding to Moody's presentation of God's love and forgiveness. God's power was evident in the little service, and there were tears on the face of this business man. As he was leaving, he was heard to say, "If God can use D. L. Moody, He can use anybody."

He was exactly right. God used D. L. Moody in a great way, in spite of all his limitations and inabilities, and God can use us, as well. What was the secret of God's power on his life and ministry? As a young convert, Moody heard a preacher say, "The world has yet to see what God can do with one man totally surrendered to Him." That night young Moody determined in his heart, "I will be that man." A detractor once said, "Does D. L. Moody have a monopoly on the Holy Spirit?" A friend who loved Mr. Moody said, "It's not that Moody has any monopoly on the Holy Spirit, but because the Holy Spirit has a monopoly on D. L. Moody."

A preacher's wife commented to me that it seems as if certain people have the power and enduement of God on their lives in an unusual way. But God's power is equally available to all of His servants, and He has a specific plan and purpose for every Christian's life. He wants to work miracles in our lives, in our families, and in our ministries, but we are not equally surrendered and obedient to His will, and dependent upon His strength and power.

I started out thinking I was a nobody in the middle of a lot of important somebodies, but I've learned that God can only use those who are willing to remain a nobody and let Him be the Somebody. I had no trouble back then realizing my own inadequacy, but it seemed to me that others were very adequate. It took me a while to realize that no one has any great power on their own, it is only when they surrender to God's power that they're used of God in a great way. While people may get caught up in the "Fame of the Name Game," God looks on hearts. He's not impressed by what seems like greatness outwardly, but He does take notice of faithfulness, willingness, and loving obedience.

I guess what God has been telling us is that if you're beautiful, talented, wealthy, worthy of honor, and filled with great potential then maybe there's little hope for you. Why? Because it's absolutely necessary to realize you can't before you can! But if the situation seems hopeless, and you have a burden on your heart to do something for God, but you know you never could, if you don't have what is necessary to do the job, then take heart! God has great things in store. He just wants us to realize that we can't do anything without Him, and then He will prove that we can do all things through Him. Christ is all in all to us. Hope for the hopeless. Help for the helpless. Love for the loveless. Worth for the worthless. Purpose for the aimless. He is all that we lack, all that we need.

Do you want to see God work in your life in a miraculous way? Do you want God to meet the pressing needs that you have? Do you know that God has burdened your heart to do some specific thing for His glory, but you're unable to do it on your own? I hope this little widow woman will bring the same kind of encouragement to your heart that she's brought to mine. Just give your little handful to God, and trust that Christ in you can do what is impossible for you to do on your own. God will use our lives greatly, even if we are unlikely choices.

Chapter Two

Life In The Balance

"That in all things he might have the preeminence."
(Colossians 1:18)

Someone once asked me, "What is the hardest thing about being an evangelist's wife?" Without a thought I answered, "Finding the right balance of everything." Though I hadn't actually weighed it out to that point before, I knew that it actually was the prevailing struggle that seems to characterize my frustration. When I think of balance I instantly imagine a comical portrait of myself weaving and wobbling, face upward, with six basketballs and a crystal vase tottering precariously on my nose and threatening to crash any second.

Though I enjoy my responsibilities, there always seems to be a tug-of-war in progress so that no matter what I'm doing I feel that I really ought to be doing something else. Just when I start to see some progress or improvement in one area I realize I am completely neglecting something else that is important. So where do you find the answer?

Immediately the Lord directed my thoughts to the book of Colossians, which has always seemed to me to be a book that centers upon Christ. Like a wheel smoothly spinning in perfect balance, it only does so because it revolves correctly around its central fulcrum, Jesus Christ. Our lives as Christians can only find balance and run smoothly if Jesus Christ is the central thought, the central purpose, and the central aim.

"That in all things he might have the preeminence." That is the balancing principle that ought to order my priorities and plans. But how can someone like me make this practical and livable so that it brings peace and order to the hectic conflict of every day life?

Recognize The Brevity Of Life.

This is the first thing the Holy Spirit told me. *"Seeing his days are determined, the number of his months are with thee, thou hast appointed his bounds that he cannot pass;"* *(Job 14:15)* My days are already numbered by God and determined, though their number is not revealed to me. If I knew I had a short time to live and finish those things which were truly important, what would they be? What would win out in importance and what would not really matter?

David knew also that to realize how short life really is would spur him on to do the best things in service to God. *"So teach us to number our days, that we may apply our hearts unto wisdom."* *(Psalm 90:12)* God has already numbered our days. David simply prayed that God would continually remind him of that fact. When I bring it into focus, the shortness and uncertainty of life will also help me to determine the true order of priority in my own life so

24

Life In The Balance
'that in all things he might have the preeminence'.

Remember To Follow The Example Of Jesus.

I had the privilege of attending a Christian school, and in my Bible I had written a quote the basketball coach gave. "Do only what Jesus would do if He were in your shoes...He is, you know." Not only are we indwelt by God's Holy Spirit, we also have the Example of Jesus' earthly life and the exhortation to live in the same manner. *"For even hereunto were ye called: because Christ also suffered for us, leaving us an example, that ye should follow his steps:"* *(I Peter 2:21)* He didn't have a home or career to maintain, but spent every day, from early in the morning till late at night, meeting the needs of others. He didn't always please people, but He did always please God, and said, *"...the Father hath not left me alone; for I do always those things that please him."* *(John 8:29)*

In the Christ-like life, people come before things. Spiritual matters before carnal. The eternal before the temporal. Others before self. Obedience comes before any plans or goals of my own. This clarifies many priority problems quickly. I need to stop and evaluate when I am faced with a 'balancing act,' and act on the principle of what Jesus would do. This brings glory to Christ, as well as bringing order to my priorities, so *'that in all things he might have the preeminence.'*

Realize That I Will Stand Before Christ.

We all know that the Bible says we will stand before the Lord to account for the things done in our body, but I don't think we always stop to consider, "I am going to look into the face of Jesus, and answer to Him for what I am going

25

to do today... and for what I am going to do this minute." If that really became reality to us, I believe it would change a lot of what we do, play by play.

We will give account for what we don't do as well, because of poor and unspiritual priorities. A lack of balance in our life will cause the 'best' things to get pushed out by the 'good' things, and before we know it we will have missed the mark for which we are aiming, the 'high calling of God in Christ Jesus.'

Someone has said, "You have 24 hours each day to use in any way you choose, and you are the sum total of how you use those hours." How I use my time determines whether I am a loyal, faithful servant to God, or a disobedient backslider. It determines whether I am a good wife and mother, or neglect my children and home-making responsibilities.

Dr. R. G. Lee left us this advice. "If you had a bank that credited your account each morning with $86,400, that carried no balance from day to day, allowed you to keep no cash in your account, and finally every evening cancelled whatever part of the amount you had failed to use during the day, what would you do? Draw out every cent, of course! Well, you have such a bank and its name is 'TIME.' Every morning it credits you with 86,400 seconds. Every night it rules off, as lost, whatever you have failed to invest to good purpose. It carries no balances. Each day 'TIME' opens a new account with you. Each night it burns the records of the day. If you fail to use the day's deposits, the loss is yours."

Yesterday is a cancelled check, tomorrow a promissory note. Today is the only cash you have -- use it wisely. When I consider the reality of the Judgment Seat of Christ, and whether I will receive a "Well done, thou good and faithful servant," or a frown of disapproval, it causes me to want to balance my life in light of pleasing Him, so *'that in all things he might have the preeminence.'*

It's always easier to say than to do, and to give advice rather than take it. But the answer is available, as well as the answer to every other question we face. The principle is in the Bible, but the practice of it must be in me. With the Lord's help, maybe I can get out from under all those tottering basketballs on my nose, and find relief from the frustration of continuously juggling poor priorities.

Keeping Christ as the central purpose, ordering my daily activities and decisions so that He has the preeminence, is the only thing that will keep my LIFE IN THE BALANCE.

HIS GRACE IS SUFFICIENT

"And he said unto me, My grace is sufficient for thee for my strength is made perfect in weakness. Most gladly therefore, will I rather glory in mine infirmities that the power of Christ may rest upon me." 2 Corinthians 12:9

"My Grace Is Sufficient," He whispers to me
In times of distress, sorrow, sickness or need.
I can do nothing without Him, 'tis true,
But through Him, I'm learning, all things I can do.

A new set of trials today I must face,
Yet there comes with each one
a new measure of grace;
I have not the grace for what
tomorrow may hold
But I have His promise of grace that's untold.

Christ in His love, O its depths are unknown,
Leads me to heights I can't scale on my own.
He knows only in battles that I just can't win,
Will I learn that my strength
must come only from Him.

Cathy Corle

28

Chapter Three

I Am Resolved (Or Am I?)

"Life is a book of volumes three:
The Past, The Present, and The Yet To Be.
The first is completed and laid away,
The second we are writing day-by-day,
The next and the last of the volumes three
Is locked from sight --- God holds the key."
(Author unknown)

It all started out so simply ... I was just going to kill two birds with one stone and hunt through some old idea scraps while I sorted and threw away and filed things from old notebooks. I only meant to spend a few minutes at it...

But hours later, I found myself drowning in sheets of paper, and memories, and thankfulness, and even a few regrets. You've heard of your life passing before your eyes, right? Well, that would be an accurate description of what happened to me, though it wasn't a scrape with eternity that brought it on. It was just all those pieces of paper -- and the things I found written on them in hand-writing that looked strangely familiar -- just like mine, to be exact.

I guess I could blame it on my write-o-mania. Since the short stories in eighth grade, and poetry in high school, I am just compelled to write things down. (In spite of this compulsion, I've been awfully upset with myself more than once over things I *didn't* write down.) It might also be blamed on this nagging idea of being organized and having my life all neatly filed away in a notebook in the form of schedules, lists, priorities, reminders, etc., etc., etc. which are hopelessly beyond all hope of ever being organized OR fitting in a notebook. (I have found that organization is a lost cause for women. Men have secretaries, so they can pretend to be organized. Women are so tied up being secretaries to the men that all our stuff gets thrown into that bottomless manila folder labeled 'LATER.')

Maybe I could blame my sentimental attack on the first little scrap that fell out of my old Bible case. It was something I stuck away, planning to get it back out about now, but I had quite forgotten it. This first one was titled "My Resolutions" and it was written in my oldest daughter's 8 year old scrawl just about this time last year. It had just five items, but I thought it was quite a tall order for such a little girl to write up on her own. She said, "My Resolutions: I want to be good and obey. I want to read my Bible. I want to pray. I want to win more souls, and most important do what God wants. Lydia. My resolutions for 1991."

I found that list last January -- probably in a sock drawer or somewhere -- and put it away, planning to show it to her at the end of the year. Now that she's 9 years old, and speeding on toward 10, I can see that the list was forgotten, but the purpose was not. Though quite a normal kid, I know that she's serious about her desire to do right in these areas. While I wouldn't try to say she's never slipped up on them, I would tell you that she's quite consistent in her 'want-to.' Though I know her failings, I see them through a mother's eyes, not only seeing what she is and what she does, but also what she wants to be and wants to do. I guess that's just what the Lord wanted me to see before I was swallowed up by all those pieces of paper...

Because I could have been in for quite a shock. I found myself reading things I had written six, seven, and eight years ago, and I just stared in disbelief. "I said *that*...?" Some of it was poetry and song lyrics that never quite got finished. Some of it was the 'idea-scraps' that later turn into messages in *Revival Fires!* Many were things that the Lord was teaching me as I read through my Bible and saw something I'd always missed before. Others were principles learned in the School of Hard Knocks --- the institution from which I claim all my earned degrees!

Some were things I'd written only to myself, in discouragement, in preparation for something, in planning projects and events that are now a distant memory. I found myself reliving so many 'ups-and-downs' from the past several years. Some of the most discouraging and heart-breaking things I've faced found their way to a little scrap of paper to muster up some courage to keep on going and trusting the Lord. Some of the goals that I had made and then conquered were listed, with other goals I'd listed that never got past the list. Some of the most exciting and rewarding times were there in 'Praise the Lords' on the prayer lists and poems and songs. The most important things I'd learned and decisions I had made in the past ten years were right there in front of me on those pieces of paper. Victory, defeat, lessons learned, projects completed, decisions made, all right before my eyes.

I found this list that was dated April, 1983. I was 22 years old, and we had been on the road for a year and a half. Our first daughter was just a year old. It was written entirely for my benefit, so it may not read very smoothly to someone else.

My Priorities:

#1 To put God first in my life, by spending time with Him in prayer and Bible study, shaping me to be the lady He created me to be. To put God first by making my life an offering to Him in everything I do, doing and being first-class instead of mediocre. To be used in His service.

#2 "Others, Lord, yes others, let this my motto be, Lord let me live for others that I may live like Thee." Starting first with my husband, then daughter, our immediate families, and then then folks in the churches where the Lord sends us (especially preachers' wives), working out to every single individual the Lord brings across my path each day. Lord, especially let me lead souls to Christ each week.

#3 Myself, and any other responsibilities or things I want to do that don't fall under other categories. In reality I set my priorities as this: Jesus, Others, Yourself - God's formula for true joy. Lord, make me the sum total of your true joy, make it evident in my life as a testimony. I so need you for that!

My personal goals: #1 To become the feminine, ladylike version of Christ-likeness that creates an aura of sweetness, softness and purity surrounding it. To allow God to make me exactly what He created me to be, and be used in His service in exactly the way and the place He created me for. Lord, glorify Jesus through me.

#2 To bring credit to my husband and his ministry as his wife, make him proud of me and satisfy him personally. D. L. Moody once heard it said, "It is yet to be seen what God can do with one man totally surrendered." My goal for our marriage is to prove through our life together what God can do through 'one flesh,' two who are one, who totally surrender themselves and their life together to God's will.

#3 To see Lydia and any other children God gives us, (Rebekah arrived a few years after this scrap of paper!) spiritually fruitful -- saved and serving....

The next page must have been lost, but this was one of those scraps of paper that had me shaking my head, wondering, "Did I really say all that?" I must have really meant it, for I found several other lists titled "My Priorities", "My Goals", "My Resolutions for ..." While all of them mentioned some things that were on my mind at the time, many of these purposes and 'resolutions' were mentioned almost word for word in all of them. I find myself lamenting, "If only living them out were as simple as writing them down!"

On one sheet labeled, "Priorities for the Preacher's Wife," I wrote: I will never apologize or make excuse for my husband's preaching or stand on the Bible. I will never pity my children or teach them they are deprived because of being 'preacher's kids.' I will never allow the work of the ministry to replace my ministry to my family. I will never make decisions based upon money, but on principle. I will never make decisions based upon what others think, but on what the Bible says. I will never let a friend go with a need unmet if I am able to meet it. I will never back out of a decision or responsibility once I'm prayerfully sure God wants me to do it, regardless of how doubtful I am later. I will never allow the busyness of God's work to crowd out God Himself from my life." My, how many times I've had to come back to that last one!

I found schedules that never seemed to work their way into our busy schedule. (Ouch! That one hurts!) I found hundreds of "To Do" lists, dated and crossed off that read like a journal of where I went and what I did. I found lists of ideas for books to be written, tapes to be recorded, projects to be tackled. There was a list of areas of responsibility, where I was trying to narrow a million and one jobs down to several major categories, to help keep them in perspective. (Not to mention keeping them from running over me!)

There was a little scrap that said, "Bad Habits and Time Leaks," and listed all the ways I wanted to discipline myself to quit wasting time. One sheet bore the heading: "Weaknesses To Work On", another said "Is Anything To Hard For The Lord?" and still another was titled: "What Could God Do With Me?" Though they came from different notebooks and different years, all were painfully similar, listing my not-so-good points that I wanted to conquer.

I don't have to read between the lines to see that I was leaning heavily on God's promises to change me from what I was to what I should have been. *"Being confident of this very thing, that he which hath begun a good work in you will perform it until the day of Jesus Christ."* *(Philippians 1:6)* My comment was, "God won't quit or get disgusted with me."

"Now unto him that is able to do exceeding abundantly above all that we ask or think, according to the power that worketh in us..." *(Ephesians 3:20)* About that I said, "God is able to make me even more than I can imagine or hope for, but it is regulated by my surrender to the Holy Spirit's control." The bottom of the page bore this verse: *"For it is God which worketh in you both to will and to do of his good pleasure."* "God not only promised to help me do His work, but also to help me will; to desire and decide. Praise the Lord! No matter how weak-willed I am in the flesh, *"I CAN do all things through Christ which*

strengtheneth me." (Philippians 4:13)

Tozer said, "We may be known by the following: What we want most, What we think about most, How we use our money, What we do with our leisure time, The company we enjoy, Whom and what we admire, and What we laugh at. These are a few tests. The wise Christian will find others."

I guess I learned some things about myself from those little scraps of paper. One thing I know: had I subjected myself to a full evening of unreached goals and unmet ideals in earlier days, I would have ended the episode in a tearful crisis. But time and reality have helped me to look at all the things that DID come to pass. All the prayers that were answered. All the goals that were met and projects that were finished. All the ideals, while still crude and imperfect in their nitty-gritty, everyday-life form, are nevertheless still the goals and ideals I want to strive for.

It's good to know that, just as I look at my daughter's resolutions, and see how hard she's tried to live up to them in spite of her failures, my Father in Heaven looks at me with the same grace, that sees not just my actions, but also my 'want to'. It's much easier to pick yourself up and go again after you've stumbled when you know that God's grace and mercy and forgiveness are unlimited.

I'm even to the point where I'm glad I'm missing on good goals, rather than reaching wrong ones. I've gotten realistic enough to thank God that it's not my life's ambition to be a bank robber! I'm sure I could be fighting against the wrong desires, instead of fighting myself to fulfill the right ones. Instead of just seeing that I haven't made the mark and chalking my life up to complete failure, I can see the fact that I'm making some progress. Even though it's slow progress, it's still in the right direction. What a glorious day in my life when I realized that all those goals and priorities and ideals and resolutions were not pass-or-fail checklists, but a target to help me know how to aim.

I also learned that I'm becoming more realistic in my goals - trying to bite off smaller bits from the dream of the future instead of choking on it all at once. A list that said, "1989 Goals" had far fewer and smaller items, though I haven't completely abandoned the previous ones. I think I'm just learning to tackle them in smaller segments. At the top of that list I found: "Learn to praise the Lord sincerely everyday of my life. Be faithful in prayer, Bible study, and soulwinning. Discipline in schedule and weight. (Ouch, again.) Control my thoughts and my words."

Then there were declarations of a new era or new principle of thought in my life -- and many of them were real turning points for me. Here is one of those: "Happiness is not an emotional euphoria in response to a set of pleasing circumstances. Happiness is a decision -- an act of the will. Happiness is putting those you love first and forgetting your own petty fears and sorrows. Happiness is risking your heart without fearing rejection, giving yourself without holding back. Happiness is knowing and accepting who you are and why God made you, and yes, exulting in it. Happiness is closing the door forever on the guilt and remorse and heartbreaks of the past and not letting them mar the beautiful reality of life's most important day -- Today. Happiness is putting to rest all the fears and forebodings of the future and refusing to let Tomorrow's rain cloud up Today's sunshine. Happiness is believing and practicing the love and omnipotence of God. He has control of tomorrow, and His only purpose is to love me through every trial and triumph He allows. Happiness is the freedom to smile, to think, to love, and to give that I have desperately searched for in a feeling, when all along it awaited me in a decision. Lord, You decided for me to be happy when you made me and when you saved me. I decided for me to be happy Today."

Every year you hear people arguing about New Year's Resolutions that they aren't going to bother making since they never last beyond January, yet I wonder --- if we never decided to do *many* good and right things, would we ever go on to accomplish *any* good and right things? Maybe there is some value in making goals, and ideals, and priorities and resolutions, whether you do it in January or any other month of the year. If it did no other good, it certainly serves the purpose to teach you a few things about what you really are. I guess I've learned that from all my little scraps of paper.

Well, here it is January again, and I feel this urge to write down some fresh new ideas, some goals of things I'd like to accomplish, some lessons the Lord has been writing in my heart. I doubt if I could let it go by without writing SOMETHING! If I aim well, and work hard, I expect to see a few more of those items crossed off the list during this year. And I hope to become a lot more like that description I found in my old notebook, which I also hope will make me a little more like the description I found in God's book of Proverbs, chapter 31.

I AM RESOLVED, and with the Lord's help, surrendered to His power, committed to His purposes, I'm confident that I'll get to see some more of those dreams coming true.

Rejoicing In The Shadow

Because thou hast been my help, therefore, in the
shadow of thy wings will I rejoice."
Psalm 63:7

I will rejoice in the shadow
When there's darkness in my way,
For I know the Heavenly Father
Walks beside me day by day.

And if my path be hidden
Illumined not by light above,
It's not because He has forsaken;
It's the shadow of His love.

So now when faced with darkness
I can trust instead of fear,
Since I know His shelt'ring shadow
Means He's more than ever near.

And because He's ever near me,
And His grace has been my choice,
He will guide me through the darkness;
In His shadow I'll rejoice.

—   Cathy L. Corle

Chapter Four

The Importance of One Woman

In the 1990's, Christian ladies tend to feel lost in the crowd. Depression and a lack of self-esteem seem to plague the feminine role. ERA and humanism have programmed us to think that there is little value in being 'just a housewife' and that our position as ladies is second-rate.

The devil plays upon that lack of understanding to tell us, "It won't make that much difference if you do wrong. Why you're just one person, and a woman at that! It won't matter if you miss church, if you don't teach a class, if you don't do your part. You're only one woman -- how much difference could you possibly make?"

The Bible gives us a quite different perspective, however, concerning the importance of one woman. Rather than being 'just another number,' women throughout the Bible have made a difference, and their role in the plan of God teaches us many things about THE IMPORTANCE OF ONE WOMAN.

The Importance Of One Woman's Soul

The account of John chapter 4 relates to us the importance of one woman's soul. *"Then cometh he to a city of Samaria, which is called Sychar... Now Jacob's well was there. Jesus therefore, being wearied with his journey, sat thus on the well: and it was about the sixth hour. There cometh a woman of Samaria to draw water: Jesus saith unto her, Give me to drink... Then saith the woman of Samaria unto him, How is it that thou, being a Jew, askest drink of me, which am a woman of Samaria? for the Jews have no dealings with the Samaritans. Jesus answered and said unto her, If thou knewest the gift of God, and who it is that saith to thee, Give me to drink; thou wouldest have asked of him, and he would have given thee living water."* (John 4:5-10)

The Lord Jesus Himself thought it important enough to take an entire day out of His short ministry and walk miles out of His way to share the message of salvation with just one woman. One of the greatest salvation messages He ever preached was to this one woman at the well of Sychar.

But why was she so important to Jesus? Did she have something that we cannot hope to have, that the Lord might care so much for us? This woman was not important because of wealth or position, else she would not have been at the well drawing her own water. The importance of her soul was not due to character or moral purity, because this woman had experienced the depths of sin, and was even now living in an adulterous relationship. *"The woman answered and said, I have no husband. Jesus said unto her, Thou hast well said, I have no husband: For thou hast had five husbands; and he whom thou now hast is not thy husband: in that saidst thou truly."*

If it wasn't her wealth, her position, her character and

morality -- what made her soul so valuable to Jesus? *"For what shall it profit a man if he shall gain the whole world, and lose his own soul. Or what shall a man give in exchange for his soul." (Mark 8:36-37)* One woman's soul -- every woman's soul -- is worth more than all the wealth of the world, and there is not a woman alive who is not just as important to the Lord as this Samaritan woman for whom He showed such compassion and concern. Have you realized the importance of your soul? Have you truly been born again and transferred your citizenship to Heaven? Don't take a chance on your salvation because you think you're just a number to God. Jesus died for YOU, whether you are the best or the worst in the sight of the world. Your soul is important and valuable to God.

The Importance Of One Woman's Soulwinning

When this woman believed on Jesus, she immediately proved to us the importance of one woman's soulwinning. Single-handedly, this one woman turned her entire town upside-down with the Gospel. This she accomplished without the aid of one memorized verse, a plan of salvation, or any Bible knowledge at all. She had only the testimony of what Christ had done in her life and the new-born glow of joy and forgiveness upon her countenance. Soulwinning tools and methods are valuable and needful, but what a blessing to know that even without the help of these, the soulwinning of one woman can have such impact.

Your soulwinning is important. You say, "I couldn't make that much difference." God says that you can. Andrew could have made that excuse. He was never seen bringing the multitudes to Christ. But he was faithful to bring folks one by one, and one of those named Peter was used by God to bring multitudes. Without Andrew's faithfulness, you would never see Peter's fruitfulness. One of the most important things to realize is that God does not expect me to live up to someone else's potential, but He knows what abilities and opportunities I have, and I will someday stand before Him to give account of how I've used them.

It's exciting to me to find two groups of people in John 4 who were saved as a result of this woman's witness. Although many Samaritans were saved directly as a result of her message and her changed life, there were many more who did not believe on the basis of her testimony but were compelled to seek Christ out themselves.

"The woman...went her way into the city, and saith to the men, Come, see a man, which told me all things that ever I did: is not this the Christ? Then they went out of the city, and came unto him...And many of the Samaritans of that city believed on him for the saying of the woman...And many more believed because of his own word; And said unto the woman, Now we believe, not because of thy saying: for we have heard him ourselves, and know that this is indeed the Christ, the Saviour of the world." (John 4:28-30,39,41,42)

All of us can see people saved one on one if we are faithful to go out with the message. But we will never know the full impact of our witness until we get to Heaven and find out how many more people came to Christ later because they first heard the message from us. That will help you keep from getting discouraged! None of these folks would ever have been saved if this one woman had minimized the importance of her personal responsibility to spread the Word.

The Importance of One Woman
The Importance Of
One Woman's Surrender

This is illustrated in the life of Mary, and the verse that I claimed as my 'life verse' in high school. *"Behold the handmaid of the Lord; be it unto me according to thy word."* (Luke 1:38) Throughout history, the Almighty has chosen to use weak human vessels to accomplish his eternal purposes. Had there not been one woman with a desire to be used of God and a willingness to resign from her own dreams and desires, the story of our redemption would no doubt read much differently.

Mary was willing to sacrifice her heart's longing to establish a home with the man she loved and allow him to doubt her character and purity. Because she demonstrated her surrender of this love to the plan of God, it was miraculously given back to her. An angel stepped out of Heaven and came to the man she loved with the reassurance that she was the pure, sweet girl he had thought her to be. Even as Abraham placed his beloved Isaac upon the altar, God sometimes allows us to be tested so that we must prove our willingness to surrender even the most precious things that He has given us.

As all little girls do, one certain little girl had a motherly longing toward dolls. As she entered a toy shop with her father she immediately set her heart upon the first doll she spied. It was only a rag doll, a cheap little likeness of a baby, but in her childish heart she laid claim upon it and determined to make it her own. As her father shopped, she hugged it closely to her and soon he had decided upon his purchase and came to take her home. As soon as he reached for the little doll to place it back on its shelf, she clung to it desperately and fought with all her strength to keep it. The bewildered father soon had the doll back on its shelf and he carried home a tearful and indignant little girl.

When they arrived at home the mother greeted her little girl with a lovely cake and sang "Happy Birthday To You." The father reached into the bag he had carried from the toy shop and pulled out the most lovely doll the child had ever seen. All the while she had been clinging desperately to her cheap little rag doll, her father's only reason in taking it away was because he had something far better in store for her. So it is in the life of God's child. God always gives His very best to those that leave the choice with Him.

Your surrender is important to God. What is the desire, need, or problem in your life that you find yourself unwilling to lay at His feet? Trust His fatherly love and watchfulness to make that decision for you. Mary could tell you that God's plan is far better than our own, yet only you can make that surrender for your own life.

The Importance Of One Woman's Service

Often we are defeated by thinking that the small amount of work we can accomplish alone is insignificant, yet in Mark 14 we see a dramatic illustration of the importance of one woman's service. This woman did not preach a sermon, or write a book of the Bible, or many other things that are recognized as important. The small thing that she was able to do, however, was to render a humble service to the Lord by anointing Him with precious ointment. She gave what she had and did what she could when she had the opportunity.

In response to her service the Lord commended her by saying, ***"She hath done what she could: she is come aforehand to anoint my body to the burying...Wheresoever this gospel shall be preached throughout the whole world,*** *this also that she hath done shall be spoken of for a memorial of her." (Mark 14:8-9)* She may not have realized its importance, and those around her certainly did not understand, but Jesus did.

This one woman would not be stopped by the limitations of her capacity to serve, or by the criticism her service received from even good Christians. I guess the most important thing to see is that when you serve, you will be criticized. It wasn't the drunkards and harlots who found fault with her service to the Savior, but the disciples who should have encouraged her.

It's been said that the only way to avoid being criticized is to say nothing, do nothing, and be nothing! I guess the biggest victory we can have is to say, "I am going to serve God and never let criticism stop me. I don't know who it is who will criticize me, I don't know what they might say, but I'm going to find out what God wants me to do and do it faithfully no matter what anybody has to say." Like hers, our Christ-honoring service will live on throughout eternity.

And your influence is important. Eve was only one woman, yet her sin and the influence she had upon her husband is still being felt today. Jezebel was just one woman, but she was responsible for leading two entire nations away from God into idolatry. Someday we will see the far-reaching effects of our influence. I wonder if we will be thankful or ashamed.

Realize today the infinite importance of one woman -- the woman that lives at your house, and raises your children and is married to your husband. The woman that goes to your church and teaches your class and has a good or bad testimony before your neighbors.

Realize that your soul is important. Your soulwinning is important. Your surrender is important. Your service is important. Your influence will touch the lives of countless

45

others and determine much about the future of your family and your church.

Don't let the devil make you think it won't make any difference. He knows how much God loves you and plans to use you if you ever begin to understand THE IMPORTANCE OF ONE WOMAN.

Chapter Five

Back To Square One

"This is the day which the LORD hath made; we will rejoice and be glad in it." (Psalm 118:24)

"Brethren, I count not myself to have apprehended: but this one thing I do, forgetting those things which are behind, and reaching forth unto those things which are before, I press toward the mark for the prize of the high calling of God in Christ Jesus." (Philippians 3:13-14)

Back to "Square One" came from somewhere in my mind as I considered starting the New Year of 1999. Who knows where that statement originated. Maybe it was a master engineer or draftsman starting over with a new sheet of graph paper, or the neighborhood kids playing hopscotch. All I know is that it signifies "RESTART" (one of those computer terms you hate.) Often in life we find ourselves starting over, and the little square on your calendar that says "January 1" is as good a place as any.

Starting over. Often it's an exciting time, after one job or stage of my life is completed, and I'm going on to something new. It may be a scary time of picking up the pieces after your dreams have crumbled and figuring out where to go from here. It might be the result of a failure in some area. They say that failure is just the opportunity of getting a fresh start with a lot more experience. Thomas Edison told a discouraged co-worker while they were laboring over an invention, "We have not failed! We now know 10,000 things that don't work!"

One day it occurred to me that God was very, very gracious to grant us life in segments. My human frailty would tremble beneath the weight of my whole lifetime and life's work laid on my shoulders and on my mind at once. (My human self is especially feeble, because I can sometimes look at the list of what I need to accomplish in one day and feel overwhelmed!) Instead, the Lord hands my life to me one day at a time, one hour at a time, one task at a time, so that I can focus my attention and energy and be challenged instead of chastened. So here we are at square one again, the year 1999.

What a blessing for those who have been despairing in failure and non-productive activity! "Tomorrow is a fresh, clean, white page of my life, with no mistakes in it." I am reminded of the grace and forgiveness of God Almighty, and the miraculous reality that I can have the past erased from my account, and truly have a new beginning. *"Therefore if any man be in Christ, he is a new creature: old things are passed away; behold all things are become new." (II Corinthians 5:17) "If we confess our sins, he is faithful and just to forgive us our sins, and to cleanse us from all unrighteousness." (I John 1:9) "And their sins and iniquities will I remember no more." (Hebrews 10:17)* Square one is a place for confession.

January first is also a natural time to consider the goals and priorities you have, and to consecrate yourself anew to the job or jobs that God has for you during the coming year. In the book called The Mrs. Ministry I challenged ladies to consider every area of responsibility that God has given them the way they would expect a preacher to consider his ministry or church. With that thought in mind, what goals do I have in the coming year of my ministry as a wife, as a mother, as a church member, as a soulwinner, and as a friend? Maybe I ought to write down each of those areas, and think through what is the next step of spiritual growth for me in that area of my life, and pray over those goals. Square one is a great place for consecration.

One of the most important commitments I need to make, and the one that is the guarantee for every other commitment I make, is the promise of faithfulness. I don't know what circumstances and problems and heartaches I might face during the coming year. I don't know what might distract my attention from doing right and get me off-track. So I want to make a commitment of faithfulness, and then make that promise again to the Lord every day this year. I'd like to make it from square one to square 365 without quitting on God, and one of the surest ways to do that is to make faithfulness itself a primary concern and matter of prayer.

In our fundamental churches we stress spiritual growth and going forward and climbing higher and doing more than ever before, and there's certainly nothing wrong with that. But I'm afraid that sometimes we fail to undergird that with the foundation of faithfulness. If I can't do more than I did last year, I still shouldn't get discouraged and quit. God wants me to give my best this year just like He expected me to give my best last year. If I try to win more souls this year than I did last year and come up short, God is still pleased if I give it my best.

I want to put a premium on faithfulness in my life, and

I'm asking the Lord to help me finish the way I started, and if possible to finish better than I started. But even if I have to finish in a sub-standard fashion compared to how I started, I still want to finish. I don't want to quit. I have become consumed with the idea that I want to grow old and die still serving the Lord. I don't want to be a quitter, a stumbling-block, or an illustration in somebody's sermon about what you're not suppose to do. I want to be faithful until I get to Heaven, but I know how weak I am, and how much the devil opposes me and tries to make me want to quit. So, if I need this exhortation, I'm sure that somebody else does, too. Make faithfulness as big a priority as your new goals of bigger and better things. Make it a commitment, a promise, a vow. Square one is an important place for commitment.

Well friend, here we are, back to "Square One." It's a place of confession, consecration and commitment. It's really a pretty important location along the way to becoming what God wants me to be, and an important place to stop and have a little revival meeting between the Lord and me, myself, and I.

50

Chapter Six

When the Lord's Workers Do the Devil's Work

"I must work the works of him that sent me while it is day: the night cometh when no man can work."
(John 9:4)

Is it possible that I, who have surrendered my entire life to be spent in the Lord's work, could be giving some portion of my time and effort toward getting the devil's job done? Is it probable that many, many of the Lord's servants get tangled up in doing the devil's work? It is a shocking and sobering thought, but one that must be examined carefully. According to Scripture, what exactly is the devil's work? How might a child of God who desires to serve the Lord find himself spending his time and energy in doing the devil's work? We need to find out what happens WHEN THE LORD'S WORKERS DO THE DEVIL'S WORK.

Imagine in your mind the excitement of a basketball or football game with the fans cheering and a member of your team gets the ball. Now your team's prize player takes the ball and heads in the wrong direction, and, much to your dismay, scores for the opposing team. How would you feel or respond? I wonder what God thinks when those of us who claim to be serving Him are more successful at carrying out the jobs that only the devil cares to do. Many of us are guilty of 'scoring points' for the devil's team repeatedly, and its about time someone stops the game long enough to point out which goals belong to each team.

One of the busiest jobs that occupies the devil's time is described in Revelation 12:10 where he is called *"...the accuser of our brethren...which accused them before our God day and night."* Job chapters one and two give us one account of how the devil carries out this task. One day the Lord began to brag on Job's integrity and character, and Satan was angered by it. He began to accuse Job to God, to try to cause the Lord to question Job's motives in doing right. He declared that Job would certainly cease to be faithful if God would remove his protection and blessing. The devil did not accuse the worst person he could find, but the best -- the one in whom God delighted.

They say that the three fastest methods of getting a message out are telephone, telegraph, and tell-a-woman! Women have been the subject of many jokes about talking too much, too loud, and too fast. Though men are often as guilty, still we need to examine ourselves in this area which can so easily get out of control. Charles Spurgeon wisely said, "If all men's sins were bound into two equal bundles, one entire bundle would be sins of the tongue." Gossip, slander, criticism, complaint, angry outbursts, lying, pessimism, flattery, sowing discord -- these are all ways that we 'score points' for the devil and honor him rather than Christ.

While Satan's work is to do the accusing, the Lord's

work is very different. When Jesus met an adulterous woman in John 8, did he speak accusingly to her? Did he accuse her to the scribes and Pharisees or to God? No! He wrote on the ground, and whatever it was that He wrote silenced the accusers. Jesus did not need to accuse her, for she accused herself in her conscience, those around her accused her, and surely Satan himself accused her before God. Her need was for forgiveness and reconciliation. Jesus did not excuse her sin -- He just knew how to love sinners while hating their sin. That seems to be a hard lesson for the rest of us to learn.

Our job, if we are doing the Lord's work, is to silence the accusers, to forgive others and to reconcile them with the forgiveness of Christ. *"And all things are of God, who hath reconciled us to himself by Jesus Christ, and hath given to us the ministry of reconciliation; To wit, that God was in Christ, reconciling the world unto himself, not imputing their trespasses unto them; and hath committed unto us the word of reconciliation. Now then we are ambassadors for Christ, as though God did beseech you by us: we pray you in Christ's stead, be ye reconciled to God."* *(II Corinthians 5:18-20)*

It helps no one when we point an accusing finger or dangle condemnation over their heads. They need to hear of the forgiveness and cleansing that was purchased at Calvary, and that's the ONLY news we ought to be repeating.

Benjamin Franklin, who won the hearts of colonial America with his wit and wisdom, said, "I will speak ill of no man, not even in the matter of truth, but rather excuse the faults I hear, and upon proper occasions, speak all the good I know of everybody." It is evident in Job chapter one that there were plenty of good things to say about Job, but the devil did not mention one of them. What he did was accuse

Job of doing right things for wrong motives, and cast a shadow upon Job's sterling character and dedication to God. Beware of the person who mentions nothing good about others, but never misses anything bad. They have too much in common with the devil. They are more than likely doing the devil's work and will mislead you into the same error.

Old Mamie was a woman in a small town who had a reputation for saying something good about everybody. It became a joke and a pastime among the townspeople to try and figure out what she would say. When an old drunken thief died and was going to be buried, no one in the whole town could think of anything good about him. Everything they knew of his life and his character was corrupt. The little town was buzzing, and some were even betting whether or not Mamie would find something good to say about him. On the day of his burial, everyone got quiet when it was Mamie's turn to pass the casket. With a smile on her face she said, "My, couldn't he whistle a pretty tune?" Don't you think Mamie could teach us something?

It has been said much and practiced little: "If you have nothing good to say, then say nothing." In spite of that, many of us have the attitude, "If you don't have anything good to say -- let's hear it!" As far as many Christians are concerned, the rest of us are guilty until proven innocent. No matter how faithfully we have served God over the years and given of ourselves, someone is just itching to hear something 'juicy' about us, and they instantly believe it no matter how many times it has been repeated and revised, and in spite of the fact that there are no witnesses or evidence to support it. Since each of us knows how wicked we are in our own hearts, I guess it is a boost to our ego if we can believe that everyone else is worse.

"The words of a talebearer are as wounds, and they go down into the innermost parts of the belly." (Proverbs

18:8) Gossips have been guilty of many heinous crimes. Years ago in a small town, a misunderstanding resulted in one woman mentioning to another that she had seen a certain married man stop to talk to a single young lady along the sidewalk, though she could not hear what they said, and had never seen them together at any other time. This second woman, who had not even seen the conversation, was only too glad to have some news to tell, and she passed it on, with just a bit more drama, of course.

Within a week it was reported all over town that the two had been having a long-standing affair, and this was repeated to the young man's wife. Grief-stricken, ashamed, and hurt beyond understanding, the young wife did not even wait to ask her husband if the gossip was true. When the innocent man arrived home from work that evening, he found that his wife had taken the lives of herself and their three children in the basement. He read the note that she left explaining that since he was in love with someone else and had been unfaithful, she could not stand to share him or see the children hurt by it. Her note was the first thing he knew about the 'long standing affair,' and those gossips were guilty of murdering a happy family.

Why is it that our human nature just loves to be the first to tell the nasty news? The same people who can go for months on end and never share the good news of salvation with anyone when it would help them, will be the ones who can't wait ten minutes to repeat some bad news, that they don't know is true, that will be a hindrance and discouragement to the person they tell it to. If for no other reason, the fact that we love to tell bad news is proof beyond any doubt that we're all a bunch of sinners! In reality, if we would tell the Lord what is wrong with people as much as we tell others about it, they would probably have nothing wrong with them. They'd be near perfect if we prayed for them that much!

We somehow entertain the mistaken notion that gossip and criticism is only wrong if it is untrue. When Saul was killed in battle, fulfilling the judgment pronounced upon his sin, David lamented, *"...how are the mighty fallen! Tell it not in Gath, publish it not in the streets of Askelon; lest the daughters of the Philistines rejoice, lest the daughters of the uncircumcised triumph."* *(II Samuel 19-20)* David was pleading that this tragedy not be rehearsed in the ears of the world, for it brought reproach upon God's chosen people. Proverbs 25:26 says, *"A righteous man falling down before the wicked is as a troubled fountain, and a corrupt spring."* To advertise the sins of Christians before the world does nothing but bring further shame and reproach to the name of Christ. Like poisoned water, it cannot cause anything but harm.

If you know something that someone has been guilty of, do the Lord a service and yourself a favor and SHUT UP! Most of what we repeat does not bring one iota of glory to God, but it sure makes the devil happy when the unsaved world and immature Christians hear bad news about a brother's sin. We need to lament over sin and **'tell it not in Gath.'**

Jesus did not tell the sin of one person to another even when He knew it to be true. One Christ-like quality we would do well to imitate is the art of forgetting. *"And their sins and their iniquities will I remember no more."* *(Hebrews 10:17)* Many of us lay claim to a bad memory, but our memory works amazingly well concerning the past sins of others. Long after God has forgotten the sin of another Christian, many of us are still bringing it up for discussion.

It must be true that Christians comprise the world's only army that shoots at its own wounded. *"Brethren, if a man be overtaken in a fault, ye which are spiritual restore such an one in the spirit of meekness; considering thyself, lest thou also be tempted." (Galatians 6:1)* Many people prefer to use the method of "kick him while he's down" in dealing with a faltering Christian, yet God said to **'restore such an one.'** We desperately need to learn of the love and compassion of Christ, and allow the Holy Spirit to duplicate those qualities in our relationships with other Christians.

Rather than being an accuser, Christ's command is for us to be "forgivers," following His Example, doing His work. *"And be ye kind one to another, tenderhearted, forgiving one another, even as God for Christ's sake hath forgiven you." (Ephesians 4:32)* Likewise, when we speak condemningly of lost people and their vices, we are doing the devil's work and driving them farther from the Gospel. The Lord's work is not to accuse, but to show them the way to Christ's blood-bought forgiveness.

The statements "I just tell it like it is" and "the truth hurts" are usually just excuses for the Lord's workers who prefer to do the devil's work. I know women who pride themselves in being able to control every one around them and get what they want with their cutting, caustic words. A sharp tongue does nothing for your Christian testimony, but cut it into little pieces. There is nothing 'Christian' or 'Holy Spirit-led' about words like those.

We need to pray each day as the Psalmist did: *"Set a watch, O Lord, before my mouth; keep the door of my lips." (Psalm 141:3)* A watchman or doorkeeper was someone who was always present at the door or gate, and they inspected and approved anyone before they could pass through. If we would pray that prayer, and consciously make it our practice that every word we say must pass the Lord's inspection before we allowed it to pass from our lips, how much heartache we would save ourselves and others.

I see such a need for this in my own life, that even when I mean to be serving the Lord, thoughtless words often escape from my mouth that don't bring glory to Christ at all, and how deeply they grieve my heart and the Holy Spirit in my life. I know that many times I have keenly felt that I was living proof of the old saying: "Many things are opened by mistake, but none so often as the mouth."

Scripture warns us that ladies need to be busy in their homes so that they do not fall into the trap of becoming an 'idle tattler.' *"And withal they learn to be idle, wandering about from house to house; and not only idle, but tattlers also and busybodies, speaking things which they ought not. I will therefore that the younger women marry, bear children, guide the house, give none occasion to the adversary to speak reproachfully. For some are already turned aside after Satan."* (I Timothy 5:13-15) Idle tattlers are those who 'speak things which they ought not.' The same women in our churches that never have time to go soulwinning or visit a nursing home, or clean the church, or cook a meal for someone who is sick can spend hours upon hours on the phone or over a cup of coffee going over the preacher and the church members with a fine-toothed comb, and come up with all sorts of imagined 'transgressions' of which we are guilty. All I can say about these women is "BEWARE!" Don't be caught up in their sin.

"And whatsoever ye do in word or deed, do all in the name of the Lord Jesus, giving thanks to God and the Father by him." (Colossians 3:17) It is often illustrated that praying in Jesus' name is the same as having permission to sign His name to a check. We are not using our own buying power or reputation but His. When we do something in Jesus' name, we are saying. "I am doing for Jesus what He would do if He were here." Can we accuse and criticize in Jesus' name? No! Because Jesus would not

do it. He would stand for the accused as being 'innocent until proven guilty,' rather than believe and propagate gossip and hear-say. He would forgive and restore even those who were proven to be guilty of sin, and we should do the same.

Beware of those oft-repeated phrases like: "Have you heard..." "Can you believe..." "You'll never guess..." and even the pious, "Please pray for so-and-so because I found out..." Someone has said, "There is so much good in the worst of us and so much bad in the best of us, that it doesn't behoove any of us to talk about the rest of us." If you've been guilty of being an 'accuser of the brethren,' then you've been doing the devil's work.

I need to remind myself often of the difference between the Lord's work and the devil's work and examine just what I am accomplishing through my life. It is a tragedy of huge proportions that robs God of His rightful glory and satisfies the devil and the unsaved world immensely WHEN THE LORD'S WORKERS DO THE DEVIL'S WORK.

Why God Made A Man

How disappointed God must be
Each day that He looks down to see
Us busy racing here and there
Amidst the hurried thoroughfare.
In His work we're all consumed
Yet God, Himself, can find no room
In the stressful come and go,
And our neglect must hurt Him so.

No time for the Bible? No time to pray?
No time to spend with the Lord today?
How short we have fallen and missed the goal
Of why God made man a living soul.
For when He chose to make mankind
It was not because He couldn't find
Someone to rush and fret and strive
To help Him keep His work alive.

But rather the need of God's great heart
Was for someone to share a part
Of all His love -- For God's one lack
Was the need for someone to love Him back.
And so God made man, without sin,
To glorify and commune with Him,
To love, adore, and serve the Lord
To learn and live His precious Word.

This was the purpose of God above,
Just for someone He could love
From before the Garden to an Old Rugged Cross
God loved and desired that man not be lost.
Love created and love redeems,
Love so infinite, that it seems
God's heart must break over our great sin
When we've time for His work but no time for Him.
—Cathy Corle

60

Chapter Seven

The Lord's Handmaid

"And Mary said, Behold the handmaid of the Lord; be it unto me according to thy word..."
(Luke 1:38)

In the self-exalting, success-oriented culture of the 1990's, many of us have lost sight of a vital principle in our relationship to God. While it is true that every child of God is exceedingly precious and infinitely valuable in His sight, there is an opposite pole that must also be inserted into our thinking in order to have a Scriptural estimation of our position in His service.

God has miraculously and mercifully made us his beloved children, *"As many as received him, to them gave he power to become the sons of God, even to them that believe on his name,"(John 1:12)* and He has caused us *"to sit together in heavenly places in Christ Jesus."* *(Ephesians 2:6)* God has placed us in an exalted position in His love and grace toward us. Yet, it is our duty to place

61

ourselves in a position of humility and servitude. *"HUMBLE YOURSELVES in the sight of the Lord, and HE SHALL LIFT YOU UP."* *(James 4:10)*

It is never my part to exalt myself -- that is always to be left in God's hands. He assures me in His Word that I am precious to Him, and that He cares for me and my every need. My place in God's kingdom is an exalted and privileged one, to be sure. Even so, my duty is not to 'live the part' of royalty, though I am heavenly royalty in Christ. On the contrary, my part is to humble myself and submit to Christ as a lowly servant. It is God's part to exalt me, it is my part to humble myself.

God never said to wait for Him to humble me, He commands me to humble myself. *"HUMBLE YOURSELVES therefore under the mighty hand of God, THAT HE MAY EXALT YOU in due time."* *(1 Peter 5:6)* The oft-claimed promise of revival in 2 Chronicles 7:14 hinges on me willingly humbling myself. *"If my people, which are called by my name, shall humble themselves and pray..."*

Jesus spoke of this truth when He reproved the scribes and Pharisees. *"But he that is greatest among you shall be your servant. And whosoever shall exalt himself shall be abased; and he that shall humble himself shall be exalted."* *(Matthew 23:12)* If we try to do God's job and exalt ourselves, we are headed for sure disaster. If we don't do our part and humble ourselves, we cannot be greatly used of God in His service.

Humble yourself -- let God exalt you. Mary realized this truth. When the angel announced to her that God had highly favored her with an exalted responsibility that no other woman would ever be entrusted with, she responded immediately by humbling herself in complete surrender to the will of God. *"Behold the handmaid of the Lord; be it unto me according to thy word."* While God said she was *'blessed among women'* and *'highly favored,'* the title and position she ascribed to herself was a most lowly one -- the handmaid of the Lord.

Doule, which is the feminine counterpart of *doulos,* is the Greek word rendered 'handmaid.' This term was originally the lowest term in the scale of servitude, and also came to mean *'one who willingly gives himself up to the will of another.'* Mary again uses this humbling term to speak of herself in verse 48, as she acknowledges the fact that God has so wonderfully exalted her. *"For he hath regarded the low estate of HIS HANDMAIDEN: for, behold, from henceforth all generations shall call me blessed."* God exalted her to a high privilege and position, she humbled herself to the lowest degree of surrender and servitude, and her life was mightily used of God.

In our quest to be usable and useful to God in this generation, we as ladies must learn to do just as Mary did. We must accept the marvelous fact that God has made us His precious children, princesses in the family of the King of kings, and then humble ourselves as His lowly servants. The world delights in rulership, and yet the Lord set the example for us that *"...he (or she) that is greatest among you shall be your servant."* He said, *"And whosoever will be chief among you, let him be your servant: Even as the Son of man came not to be ministered unto, but to minister, and to give his life a ransom for many."* (Matthew 20:27-28)

A Handmaid Sets Aside Her Own Projects And Goals For The Work Of Her Master.

A handmaid didn't cook her own meal until the master's meal had been served. She did not mend her own clothing until the master's belongings were in perfect repair. While we say we want to serve the Lord, few of us are willing to set aside our own things to care for the things of God. It is sorely evident in many of our churches that we are so busy with our own things that we take no time for the work of the Lord.

We are commanded to set aside our own plans for the plan of God, our own desires for the desire of God, our own will for the will of God. *"But seek ye first the kingdom of God, and his righteousness; and all these things shall be added unto you."* *(Matthew 6:33)* I may say I'm a servant of God, but have I set aside my own things to care for the things of God?

A Handmaid Lives And Works For The One Purpose Of Pleasing Her Master.

The world's philosophy assures us that 'you can't please everyone so you've got to please yourself,' to which Christ replies, *"...the Father hath not left me alone; for I DO ALWAYS THOSE THINGS THAT PLEASE HIM."* (John 8:29) Certainly living to please everyone will result in pleasing no one and end in a nervous break-down, but few of us stop to realize that living to please ourselves will end up with nearly the same outcome. In his later years, Solomon lived to make himself happy and became one of the most unhappy people on the face of the earth. The book of Ecclesiastes records his fruitless search for satisfaction.

Only in living to please the Lord can anyone find true fulfillment and pleasure. *"Servants, be obedient to them that are your masters according to the flesh, with fear and trembling, in singleness of heart, as unto Christ; Not with eyeservice, as menpleasers; but as the servants of Christ, doing the will of God from the heart; With goodwill doing service, as to the Lord, and not to men:"* (Ephesians 6:5-7) There ought to be a hunger - a deep abiding desire - to please the Lord, to win his smile and commendation, to hear him say, *"Well done, thou good and faithful servant."* I may call myself a servant of God, but am I living and working and doing everything I do striving to please only God?

The Handmaid Is Constantly Looking For And Listening For Her Master.

"Behold, as the eyes of servants look unto the hand of their masters, and as the eyes of a maiden unto the hand of her mistress; so our eyes wait upon the Lord our God, until that he have mercy upon us." (Psalm 123:2) In just such a manner, we should be seeking His face and looking for His coming, and listening to His voice as His Spirit and His Word speaks to our hearts. As far as listening for His voice we are instructed, *"But be ye doers of the word, and not hearers only, deceiving your own selves."* (James 1:22) To listen with our heart is to obey.

To watch for his coming, also means to obey. *"Who then is a faithful and wise servant, whom his lord hath made ruler over his household, to give them meat in due season? Blessed is that servant whom his lord when he cometh shall find so doing."* (Matthew 24:45-56) Our Master will soon be returning at an undesignated hour, and we want to be found busy and obedient when He comes.

The Handmaid Is Not Assigned To Mighty Noble Works, But To Lowly Tasks.

We often find ourselves as ladies not preaching great, oratorical sermons or receiving the spotlight for great deeds, but doing the menial and unnoticed work. Alan Redpath told of a lady he knew who hung a sign above her kitchen sink that read: "Divine service is conducted here three times daily."

Many ladies have felt similarly that their duties in the ministry of marriage and motherhood as well as the ministry of the church were carried out for the Lord, and rightly so. ***"Inasmuch as ye have done it unto the least of these my brethren, ye have done it unto me."*** *(Matthew 25:40)* When we serve others out of love for Christ, we truly are serving Him.

Lord of all pots and pans and things,
Since I've no time to be
A saint by doing lovely things,
Or watching late with Thee,
Or dreaming in the dawnlight,
Or storming Heaven's gates,
Make me a saint by getting meals
And washing up the plates.

Although I have a Martha's hands
I have a Mary's mind;
And when I black the boots and shoes,
Thy sandals, Lord, I find.
I think of how they trod the earth,
Each time I scrub the floor.
Accept this meditation, Lord,
I haven't time for more.

Warm all my kitchen with Thy love,
And light it with Thy peace;
Forgive me all my worrying,
And make my grumbling cease.
Thou who didst love to give men food,
In a room or by the sea,
Accept this service that I do--
I do it unto Thee.
(Selected)

Though often our service to the Lord is in serving others, let's do it heartily, *'as to the Lord, and not unto men,'* *(Colossians 3:23)* and seek to please Him in all that we do. God has highly exalted us, now it is our part to humble ourselves and surrender our lives to carry out His will and work. Such is the plan of God for THE LORD'S HANDMAID.

A SERVANT'S PRAYER

Where is there a need that I can fill?
A place to serve, to do God's will?
Where can I find some soul in distress
And offer words of comfort and rest?

Where is there some task
no one wants to do?
Master, I am willing to do it for You.
I have not as much to give as the rest,
But I can give each day my very best.

Where is the place of service
meant for me,
The job for which You created me to be?
Savior, only let me hear Thy call,
To Thyself I gladly give my all.

Let me labor, now I humbly ask,
In some great work or small
and humbling task
From dawn of day until life's setting sun,
That I may only hear from Thee, "Well done."

—Cathy Corle

Chapter Eight

Be Careful Little Heart What You Want!

Someone said that a person may be known by what he says, what he loves, what he laughs at, and what he wants. Your wants determine your pursuits. Your pursuits determine your direction. You will accomplish only those things that you want enough to work for them. What you want is pretty important, wouldn't you say?

All the sin and heartache and suffering and death that the world has ever known started with a woman who allowed herself to want the wrong thing. Look with me at Genesis chapter three. *"Now the serpent was more subtil than any beast of the field which the Lord God had made."* He was subtil, sly, and sneaky. He knew how to talk his way around anybody.

"And he said unto the woman..." My first question is: Why did he speak to the woman instead of the man? He must have known that the woman was more vulnerable to his lies, and that she was the inroad to the man. In I Timothy 2:14 we read: *"And Adam was not deceived, but the woman being deceived was in the transgression."* So the devil picked Eve as his target. Remember that we're talking about the best woman who ever lived, not the worst. She was the only perfect and sinless woman to ever breathe God's air and walk on His earth.

Yet the devil was able to use the best woman who ever lived to commit the costliest sin that was ever committed. Why? Her first mistake was listening to the devil. If she had not allowed the devil to place a question mark in her mind, she would not have fallen for his lies. Don't give the devil a hearing. He comes to every one of us every day with his lies. "If only you had this. If only you didn't have to do this. You could be happy if..." He's there every day, whether you're listening to him or not, introducing doubts, fears, complaints, and lies. When you're weak, he'll be there. The first time you give him a hearing, you're going to regret it for the rest of your life.

"...Yea, hath God said, Ye shall not eat of every tree of the garden?" The devil didn't add or subtract here. He only placed a question mark where God had placed a period. If you allow the devil to cause you to question God's word, you're definitely in trouble. If Eve had been able to say with confidence, "Yes, God did say," the confrontation could have ended immediately. But the best woman God ever made, a woman who walked with God and fellowshipped with Him in person, brought sin upon the whole world because she was unsure of the Word of God. No woman in this world can afford to be unfamiliar and

uncertain when it comes to the Bible. Your life depends on it, and so do the lives of your husband and children, and everyone that you love. You've got to spend time in the Book, and read it and memorize it and know it for yourself.

"And the woman said unto the serpent, We may eat of the fruit of the trees of the garden: But of the fruit of the tree which is in the midst of the garden, God hath said, Ye shall not eat of it, neither shall ye touch it, lest ye die." Eve's second big mistake was in not knowing for sure what God's Word had to say on the subject. She added to the Word of God. People add to God's Word about many things. "Neither shall ye touch it" may be okay as a rule, but it's unscriptural as a doctrine, simply because God didn't say it. We sometimes have rules for ourselves or our children that are wise, because they keep us a step away from sin. But people who are not grounded in the Bible might take those rules or principles that are wise protection and turn them into a man-made doctrine. We've got to be careful to distinguish between Bible doctrine and our own preferences, even when they're right. The Bible condemns the practice of 'teaching for doctrine the commandments of men.'

Once the devil knew he had her tied in knots about what God had said, he became even more bold in his attack. *"And the serpent said unto the woman, Ye shall not surely die: For God doth know that in the day ye eat thereof, then your eyes shall be opened, and ye shall be as gods, knowing good and evil."* Now the devil pulls out his all-time favorite. He's been telling this lie to every generation since Eve, and it's still working. "God's holding out on you. He's holding you back, keeping you down. God knows that if you eat this fruit you'll be on the same plane with Him, and He doesn't want you to have this because He's selfish. He knows it would make you happy, but He doesn't love you enough to want you to be happy. God's

71

keeping something away from you, but you ought to have it anyway. This is something good that could make you happy, and you deserve to have it. God's depriving you."

How many teenagers have bought into the lie of the devil? "Your parents are just trying to ruin your fun. They're old, boring, and stuck in the mud, and they want to keep you stuck in the same rut they're in. If you really want to have fun in life, you have to break away from your parents' rules and do what you want." How many kids have wrecked their lives because they believed the devil's lie, only to find out too late that their parents were trying to save their fun for the rest of their lives, instead of throwing it away for a whim?

Women all over this country are believing the devil's lies. "If you would just break free from that husband that's making your life miserable. You don't need him anyway. If only you had that other man. You could have all the love and affection and attention your heart craves. He could really make you happy." What you could really have is all the heartache and sorrow and pain and disillusionment that sin brings, and it's sure to be yours if you buy into the devil's lies. He's whispering in your ear, and if you don't stop listening to him, you're headed for heartache.

"And when the woman saw that the tree was good for food, and that it was pleasant to the eyes, and a tree to be desired to make one wise, she took of the fruit thereof..." It sounds to me like she spent too much time looking at what she already knew God did not intend for her to have. "Be careful little eyes what you see" needs to be the verse that precedes, "Oh, be careful little heart what you want." If you never see it, you'll never want it. Lot cast his eyes toward Sodom, pitched his tent toward Sodom, and then moved right in to Sodom. David saw, then he lusted, then he took. Eve took too much time to consider what was

forbidden to her. Put your blinders on. Refuse to consider whether or not you want what God already said you should not have. Once she took time to look at it, it wasn't long until she was eating it.

We want to jump into the story and say, "Eve, look at what you've got. You have a perfect and beautiful home. You've got the only perfect marriage and perfect husband in history. Things are happy, wonderful; there's nothing that you could complain about. Just look at what you have." But Eve had her eyes on what she didn't have. There were many trees that belonged to her. She could eat from every tree except one. That one belonged only to God. What she did have was much greater than what she didn't have. As a loving Father, God had good reason for what she didn't have, whether she understood it all or not. But Eve got her eyes on what she didn't have, which is covetousness, instead of having her eyes on what she did have, which results in thankfulness and contentment.

"...she took of the fruit thereof, and did eat, and gave also unto her husband with her; and he did eat." Here we see the follower step into the lead, and destruction and grief followed. No matter how poor the leadership may be, the follower must stay in position. My husband has often used the illustration of our truck and trailer. The trailer is more valuable than the truck and in many ways more important than the truck. But if the trailer ever gets in the lead, it's going to destroy itself and everything in it's path. Why? Because it was designed to follow.

The same is true in every kind of relationship: husband-wife, parent-child, and pastor-people. The follower must not try to get in the lead. Your husband listens to you, no matter how convinced you are that he never hears a word you say. You have much more influence than you would ever imagine. What is he hearing from you everyday?

73

Complaint, discontentment, fear, doubt, unspiritual advice? The fall of man was caused by a woman, and the fall of many more men has been caused by women, as well. We've got to be careful that we don't try to get in the lead. It's right to pray and ask God to lead my husband in a certain direction, wait for God to answer, and then for me to follow my husband as he follows the leadership of God. It's wrong for me to get in front and try to lead him myself.

Now we get back around to where we started. Be careful little heart what you want. Your want-to is all important. What you desire is a great indicator of what you are. It might be appropriate to say, "What you want is what you are"; at least it proves what you are.

Not only that, but what you want is an even greater factor in what you will become. Your desires and goals are an important 'direction-determiner' in your life. There are purifying goals, and there are corrupting goals.

Consider this illustration: Money is a corrupting goal, even to good people. The Bible teaches clearly that money itself is not evil, but the love of money is the root of all evil. Providing for the needs of your family is a purifying goal. If you're truly concerned about the needs of your family, that will include their spiritual needs as well as their physical needs. A person may be headed toward the goal of becoming wealthy, or they may be motivated by trying to meet all of the needs of their family. Now both of those goals may lead to you taking the same job and bringing home the same paycheck, but sooner or later there will be a fork in the road. Eventually, your goals will lead you to an end of good or evil. Many good, godly people have been shipwrecked when they allowed money-making to become their goal in life.

Raising your children to be upright, honest, good, clean-living, and Bible-oriented is a purifying goal. A lady was telling me about her husband's salvation, and it prompted me to meditate on this idea. She said her husband was an unsaved man who had been raised in an ungodly home. His childhood had been surrounded by drunkenness, hate, and an anti-Christian philosophy. When she got saved and got into a good church, he was totally disinterested in salvation, but she was surprised to learn that he wanted very much for his children to be enrolled in the Christian school.

Why? He had a desire to provide the kind of upright, clean, honest, hard-working example and environment for his children that he had missed while he was growing up. Because of this desire, and all his involvement through the years with the activities and programs at the Christian school, he eventually did get saved, and today is a faithful deacon and bus worker. Even as an unsaved man, he had a good, godly goal, and it had a purifying effect on his life.

What you want is so important. The desires of your heart determine the direction of your life. Next we'll take a closer look at how important it is for ladies to 'be careful little heart what you want'.

Remember once again that all the sin, heartache, suffering, and death that the world has ever known started with a woman who allowed herself to want the wrong thing. In part one we looked at Eve in her confrontation with her wrong desires, and how the devil was able to use her want-to to destroy all that she REALLY wanted. What you want is so important. The desires of your heart determine the direction of your life. Let me share with you a few observations about desires.

#1 The Devil Works To Make Us Want What God Has.

Like Eve, the devil has us where he wants us when he is

able to create in us a desire to have what God has. There are some things that belong only to God. It's wrong for us to strive to get what God has.

#2 *God Instructs Us To Strive To Be What He Is.*

Instead of wanting what God has, we're suppose to concentrate our time and attention and effort toward becoming what God is. That's called godliness. That's called Christ-likeness. That is to be our desire and our goal and our pursuit. It's wrong to strive to get what God has. But it's right to strive to become what God is.

#3 *When I'm Striving To Become What God Is, I Can Be Satisfied With What I Have.*

"Godliness with contentment is great gain" -- worth more than any possessions we could obtain. It's been said that, "Contentment is the art of enjoying what you have."

#4 *When I'm Striving To Become What God Is, And Satisfied With What I Have, Then God Will Bless Me With Some Of What He Has.*

There are many things that don't belong to me, and it would be wrong for me to try to get those things that are God's. But if I'll be faithful and true, God says He will

76

bless me with some of what He has. Many sins are those which stem from us trying to get what God has. Let me give you a few examples.

ALL POWER, CONTROL, AUTHORITY, AND DOMINION BELONG TO GOD
"...Thine is the kingdom, and the power, and the glory for ever. Amen." (Matthew 6:13)

Power over life and death is something that belongs only to God. *"...he giveth to all life, and breath, and all things;" (Acts 17:25)* When a human being tries to take control over this power, it is infinitely wicked. Yet today more than ever before we hear about abortion, euthanasia, assisted suicide, and every other kind of drive toward death. This is something that belongs only to God, and when a human being tries to take over in this area, it is wrong.

But God has control and dominion in other areas, as well. Power over people's lives and hearts and minds, for instance. How much conniving, manipulating, politicking, and hypocrisy come from the attempt to control other people. That is not my job. I have enough trouble trying to govern myself, or keep myself under the Lord's control.

Dominion, or the right to rule, is another form of this power that belongs to God. How many ministries have suffered in the midst of a power struggle, everyone grasping for the reins, everybody wanting to 'call the shots' and be the 'head honcho'. Now, God often calls people to a position of leadership where they do have a certain amount of influence and control in the lives of others once they have proven themselves faithful. But that desperate grasping for control and authority and power is something that God does not approve or bless.

The Bible is clear that God-ordained leadership is given

for the purpose of serving others and meeting their needs. *"For though I should boast somewhat more of our authority, which the Lord hath given us for edification, and not for your destruction, I should not be ashamed;"* *(II Corinthians 10:8)* Authority is never granted to be used in a selfish way just to benefit the leader, or to be a dictator. It's purpose is to build up and strengthen the follower. *"Neither be ye called masters: for one is your Master, even Christ. But he that is greatest among you shall be your servant."* *(Matthew 23:10-11)* We need to realize that total power and authority and dominion belong only to God, and not allow the devil to entice us to pursue it for ourselves.

ALL KNOWLEDGE BELONGS TO GOD
"For my thoughts are not your thoughts, neither are your ways my ways, saith the Lord." *(Isaiah 55:8)*

There are some things that God knows that He has chosen for us not to know, one of which is the time of His return. *"And he said unto them, It is not for you to know the times or the seasons, which the Father hath put in his own power."* *(Acts 1:7)* There are other things that God has allowed us to know something about, but has not permitted us to have complete knowledge. *"For now we see through a glass, darkly; but then face to face: now I know in part; but then shall I know even as also I am known."* *(I Corinthians 13:12)*

We often feel like we need to be in possession of all knowledge about what's going on, because that gives us some feeling of control, and we feel less vulnerable. Yet God doesn't choose for me to know everything. That is an area where He often demands that I trust Him, since He knows everything that I don't know. So much gossip and meddling and busybody activities stem from our

78

unrighteous desire to be a know-it-all. We can't stand for something to be going on and us not know all the gory details.

It's not wrong to pursue wisdom and understanding; I'm commanded to. *"Get wisdom, get understanding: forget it not; neither decline from the words of my mouth."* *(Proverbs 4:5)* But it is wrong to covet knowledge not meant for me. I don't have to be 'in the know' about everybody and everything. I'll be much better off if I can learn to mind my own business.

For example, I may feel that something might go on that could hurt myself or my family or my church, and it's very human to start being suspicious and playing the investigator all the time. But I need to remember that God knows all events and actions of others, whether it's happening right under my nose or on the other side of the world. God knows the past, present, and future that are unknown to me. God knows all the secret thoughts of the heart, of myself and of others, as well as all the words that are spoken and deeds that are done.

If there is something that God decides I need to find out, He is very capable of bringing it to my attention. But if I don't trust God with this area of all knowledge, and admit that I don't need to be a possessor of every tidbit of news, then I can very easily become a nosy busybody.

"But the Comforter, which is the Holy Ghost, whom the Father will send in my name, he shall teach you all things, and bring all things to your remembrance, whatsoever I have said unto you." *(John 14:26)* For the Holy Spirit to teach and remind me of all things necessitates that He know all things, and He does. God is omniscient, but I am limited in knowledge. Yet we don't need to worry about what we don't know, only be concerned with being in tune with the Holy Spirit. He will teach us all we need to

know, and He knows everything. He knows what is going to happen, what others are doing and saying and thinking, you name it.

The area where the Lord spoke to me about this truth is that God knows the dangers that lie ahead for us. One day one of my children put the car into gear and could have very easily killed me, because I was standing outside, and my children were inside the car and could have been injured, as well. Before I realized what had even happened, I had already jumped into the car and put my foot on the brake, and I really didn't even know what was going on. It was very real to me that day that the Holy Spirit prompted my actions, and protected me. Everything I don't know, He knows. He'll protect me and guide me if I will let Him. My pursuit should not be to know everything that has happened or will happen, but to know the Lord in a close relationship and let the Holy Spirit's guidance and protection be a reality in my life.

ALL GLORY BELONGS TO GOD
"I am the Lord: that is my name: and my glory will I not give to another..." (Isaiah 42:8)

It's so very human to want to be important to others, and our flesh very much wants to take its place at the top. But Christ's teachings are plain: Take the lower place and let God promote you. ***"And he put forth a parable to those which were bidden, when he marked how they chose out the chief rooms; saying unto them, When thou art bidden of any man to a wedding, sit not down in the highest room; lest a more honourable man than thou be bidden of him; And he that bade thee and him come and say to thee, Give this man place; and thou begin with shame to take the lowest room. But when thou art bidden, go and sit down***

80

in the lowest room; that when he that bade thee cometh, he may say unto thee, Friend, go up higher: then shalt thou have worship in the presence of them that sit at meat with thee. For whosoever exalteth himself shall be abased; and he that humbleth himself shall be exalted."

It's my job to humble myself -- it's God's part to exalt me to the position He has chosen for me to fill. *"Humble yourselves in the sight of God and he will lift you up." "It is not good to eat much honey: so for men to search their own glory is not glory." (Proverbs 25:27)* The self-exalting, bragadocious, blow-your-own-horn type of people are definitely not following the example of the Lord who *"...made himself of no reputation, and took upon him the form of a servant, and was made in the likeness of men: And being found in fashion as a man, he humbled himself, and became obedient unto death, even the death of the cross." (Philippians 2:7-8)*

All glory belongs to God. If I'll take the lowest position for myself, and just do my best to obey the Lord, He has promised to exalt me in due time, and give me a portion of that which belongs to Him. *"And whosoever shall exalt himself shall be abased; and he that shall humble himself shall be exalted." (Matthew 23:12)*

I think I've given you an idea of where I'm headed. These are things that belong only to God. I am not to allow myself to desire or seek them for myself, because they belong to God. Another area would be that of passing judgment. Judgment belongs to God. It's His job, not mine. *"Judge not, that ye be not judged. For with what judgment ye judge, ye shall be judged: and with what measure ye mete, it shall be measured to you again." (Matthew 7:1-2)*

Another item that belongs in God's possession is vengeance for wrongs done to me. *"Dearly beloved, avenge not yourselves, but rather give place unto wrath: for it is written, Vengeance is mine; I will repay, saith the Lord. Therefore if thine enemy hunger, feed him; if he thirst, give him drink: for in so doing thou shalt heap coals of fire on his head." (Romans 12:19-20)* It's not my job to make sure someone pays for what they did to me that was wrong. Getting even is not Christ-like. God knows how to even the score, leave it in his hands.

Along the same line of thought, God has all riches. *"The earth is the Lord's, and the fulness thereof: the world, and they that dwell therein." (Psalm 24:1)* He owns the cattle on a thousand hills, He owns the hills, and the gold under the hills. All riches and treasures belong to God, and His storehouse of resources are unlimited. That is why Philippians 4:19 is such an exciting promise, because there is no limit to God's ability and resources to supply my needs and answer my prayers. *"But my God shall supply all your need according to his riches in glory by Christ Jesus."* All my needs can't even begin to exhaust all God's riches.

But riches should never become my goal. I should try to be right, not rich. Money is not evil, but the love of money is the root of all evil, the Bible clearly tells us. Someone said that money is a wonderful servant and a terrible master. Covetousness leads to other sins. We need to keep money in its proper perspective, whether we have little or much of it. *"But thou shalt remember the Lord thy God: for it is he that giveth thee power to get wealth, that he may establish his covenant which he sware unto thy fathers, as it is this day." (Deuteronomy 8:18)*

God knows what He can trust me with, and what I am ready to handle. I'm sure that one of the reasons we sometimes don't have as much money as we think we ought to have is because God knows it would be dangerous to us.

82

"...the prosperity of fools shall destroy them." (*Proverbs 1:32*) The same reason why I don't give the car keys to a five year old child is why God sometimes does not entrust us with more in the area of finances. When I cease trying to grasp for money, and concentrate on becoming more godly, God has promised to bless me with some of the riches that He has in His possession.

These are all things that God has. I should not make it my goal or priority to obtain what belongs to God. The devil will be working overtime to try to cause me to desire the things that I should not be striving after.

Instead I should have my eyes set on the goal of becoming more of what God is. God is righteous, holy, and just. God is loving, kind, good, and benevolent. God is forgiving. God is patient and longsuffering. God is wise. God is a caring, compassionate needmeeter, always looking to the needs of others. It won't take me long to think of many of the qualities and characteristics of God that He wants me to try to incorporate in my own life. That is what godliness and Christ-likeness is all about. Christian means 'a little Christ' or 'copy of the original.' So the more I become like Him, however faint the resemblance may be, the more glory I bring to His name.

If I will strive to become what God is, God will bless me with what He has. My focus and goal should not become to get for myself what God has. My goal should be to try to become more like what God is. Then I can be satisfied with what I have, and more than that, God can bless me with a measure of what He has.

But how can I pursue this goal of becoming what God is? Well, here are a few ideas that come to mind immediately. Bible reading puts at our disposal God's Word and thoughts and judgments. 'Opinion' is not the word to use about what God has to say about things, since opinions

83

differ with people and can be wrong, and God's principles and judgments are absolute. But it does express the idea of what God thinks about a certain subject, so in that way, we can find out God's 'opinion' about a subject just by digging into the truth contained in His word.

"We have the mind of Christ," the Bible says. How can that be possible? God has put it in print, that we can 'read His mind'. Philippians 2:5 says that we are to let the mind of Christ control our minds. *"Let this mind be in you which was also in Christ Jesus..."* Again in I Peter 4:1, we are instructed that there is spiritual protection in this warfare with Satan by having our minds under the Lord's control. *"For as much then as Christ hath suffered for us in the flesh, arm yourselves likewise with the same mind:..."* Equip yourself with the Bible. The Bible is not just to be a book to us, or a manual on how to live, it is to become a part of us. *"Wherefore lay apart all filthiness and superfluity of naughtiness, and receive with meekness the engrafted word, which is able to save your souls."* *(James 1:21)* Just as a branch is grafted to a tree, and becomes a living, functioning part of that tree, let the Bible become an integral part of your life and thinking and decision making.

Prayer is another important avenue of pursuing Christ-likeness. *"Call unto me, and I will answer thee, and shew thee great and mighty things, which thou knowest not."* *(Jeremiah 33:3)* James 1:5 says, *"If any of you lack wisdom, let him ask of God, that giveth to all men liberally, and upbraideth not; and it shall be given him."* Prayer is spending time with God. It's been said often that we become like those with whom we spend the most time. You've noticed when your children come home expressing a different attitude or using a new pet phrase, and you think, "I know who they were with today." We are very much influenced by those we spend time with, and it's no different in our relationship with the Lord. Don't worry -- we won't rub off on Him, for God never changes. He might influence us though, if we spend enough time talking with Him, asking for His wisdom, and allowing His Word and His Holy Spirit to speak to us. Request, fellowship, adoration, communion, and conversation are all a part of spending time with God in prayer, and one of the benefits of prayer is not only the answers we get from God, but the change that it makes in us.

Soulwinning is a way that we can become more godly. Luke 19:10 says, *"For the Son of man is come to seek and to save that which was lost."* When I get concerned about seeking and saving the lost, then I become more like him. Soulwinning has a powerful effect in the hearts and lives of people, both in making us more others-oriented and in us having eternal values in mind, rather than just the temporary. God has made many promises to the soulwinner, both for time and eternity.

Giving is something that is central to Christianity. John 3:16 may be the most-quoted verse in the Bible. *"For God so loved ... that he gave..."* Giving is a central theme of godliness. You can't separate the thought of God and His character and qualities from the principle of giving. This is something that ought to characterize us as His children and His followers.

We should be willing to humble self, as we've already mentioned, and leave it in the hands of God to lift us up in the time and capacity that He chooses for us. Jesus did always those things that please the Father, so for me to be Christ-like I need to strive to do the same. Jesus was pure and undefiled by sin. There was no fault in Him. Though we can't be sinless, we can be pure from sin through confession and cleansing and striving to live clean and

85

right. I John 1:9 promises, *"If we confess our sins, he is faithful and just to forgive us our sins, and to cleanse us from all unrighteousness."*

Be others minded. It was said of Jesus, "He saved others, himself he cannot save." If we will get our eyes on the needs of others instead of being consumed with selfishness, it leads to joy in our hearts, as well as making us like the Lord who bought us with His blood.

I hope that these thoughts will be an encouragement to you, as well as a warning sign posted in a place where the devil is sure to try and trip us up. The devil works to make us want what God has. God instructs us to strive to be what He is. When I'm striving to become what God is, I can be satisfied with what I have. When I'm striving to become what God is, and satisfied with what I have, then God will bless me with some of what he has.

Don't be like Eve, who threw away all the wonderful things that God intended for her to have, because she allowed herself to pursue a desire for what she should not have had. Don't let your desires destroy you, but work to bring them into subjection with what God wants in your life. *"Delight thyself also in the Lord; and he shall give thee the desires of thine heart."* (Psalm 37:4)

Oh, be careful little heart what you want!

Chapter Nine

Don't Worry, Robin!

I have a confession to make -- discouragement and worry happen to be two of the besetting sins that I find myself battling with very regularly. On one occasion I was feeling very pressured by a seemingly impossible array of responsibilities and deadlines. The more I thought about it, the worse it seemed, and the lower I sank in despair.

Because I knew that my burden was growing greater at the same rate that my strength was growing smaller, I tried to practice the same thing that David did when he faced a set of circumstances much more worrisome than mine. In I Samuel 30:6 we read, *"And David was greatly distressed... but David encouraged himself in the LORD."*

I prayed as I worked and attempted to 'encourage myself', and it wasn't long before I was running for a pen and paper to write down this picturesque little tale that so clearly described what I had been doing. Well, it worked! I was encouraged, (not to mention a little amused and embarrassed, as well). I hope that sharing it here will result in a smile of encouragement to others as well.

Don't Worry, Robin!

The harried, hurried robin
Sat and stewed upon her nest
And she wearied as she worried
But there was no time for rest.
She had flustered as she flurried
From the East unto the West
Just to find a few fat worms
To feed the babies in her nest.

"We've just enough for now,
But what an endless task is mine;
For in just a few short hours
Will come another feeding time.
If I'm able then to muster
Just enough for them to swallow,
Before I get my breath
Again their bellies will be hollow!"

She added up the worms they'd eat
In just a day or two,
And the longer that she added
The greater her burden grew.
She despaired before she'd finished
And the year she'd calculated,
For all the earth with worms
Could not be so populated.

So she laid her head upon her wing
And then began to cry
For she could not bear the burden
Which upon her now did lie.
Convinced that God must be unfair,
The little robin asked,
"Lord, why give a little robin
Such a monumental task?"

"A task too great?" the Lord inquired,
"Why all you have to do
Is get the worms your brood needs now
And that is just a few.
I did not say to do the work
Of all the year ahead
Your job is just to do today
What I, the Lord, have said."

The robin paused and pondered,
And then she did recall
That the Father said He feeds the birds
Although they may be small.
So no matter how she fretted
All her worry was in vain,
For He promised that He'd feed them,
And His promise there is plain.

Herself she reprimanded,

"What wasted tears were mine,
While I struggled to supply myself
What was promised all the time!
Why fret and fume and fluster
Over every daily need?
For God told us just to seek Him first,
And the robins He would feed."

"I can't bear the future's burdens
And its tasks I cannot face,
For Tomorrow is too great a strain
On Today's sufficient grace.
But when Tomorrow becomes Today
And the future becomes the present,
I'll find His grace is again enough
To make my task seem pleasant."

"Today is all I need to see
I won't worry for Tomorrows.
Today has enough of heartaches
Without borrowing future sorrows."
Then the robin sighed in great relief
And found that she could rest
While leaving tomorrow in God's hand
And just doing today her best.

So then finally she rested
After worrying so long,
And as her peace returned

Don't Worry, Robin!
She found her long-forgotten song.
She again could sing
And bring to hearts a note of cheer
When she let her Father handle
The rest of all the year.
-Cathy Corle-

"Behold the fowls of the air: for they sow not, neither do they reap, nor gather into barns; yet your heavenly Father feedeth them. Are ye not much better than they?...your heavenly Father knoweth that ye have need of all these things. But seek ye first the kingdom of God, and his righteousness; and all these things shall be added unto you. Take therefore no thought for the morrow: for the morrow shall take thought for the things of itself. Sufficient unto the day is the evil thereof."
(Matthew 6:26,32-34)

"What shall we then say to these things? If God be for us, who can be against us? He that spared not his own Son, but delivered him up for us all, how shall he not with him also freely give us all things?"
(Romans 8:31-32)

Chapter Ten

Life Under the Magnifying Glass

"And the Lord said unto Joshua, This day will I begin to magnify thee in the sight of all Israel, that they may know that, as I was with Moses, so I will be with thee."
(Joshua 3:7)

As an evangelist's wife, one of the special privileges and joys I have is the opportunity to meet many pastors' wives all across the country. Many of my dearest friends are preachers' wives -- and I think we have some unique circumstances, and sometimes problems. My heart has been moved many times concerning the particular burdens and needs that preachers' wives have. Not surprisingly, I often find myself looking for truths from God's Word, for myself and for others, that will help us to be exactly what the Lord intends for us to be as we 'complete' our husbands in the ministry. This is one of those truths that is so encouraging. A pastor's wife in Louisiana told me recently that this message was a special encouragement to her. I hope that many ladies who serve faithfully in our churches in other areas will also be helped by this leadership principle, but it is directed especially to the many wonderful preachers' wives whom the Lord is using. I hope it will be 'just what we need.'

We've all learned that leadership has its sweet and sour moments, especially in the ministry and most especially if you are a preacher's wife. While most preachers' wives I know are glad to be in the ministry and enjoy their service to the Lord, they still find exasperating situations that they must face with their church people. Many find themselves in a position of leadership with the church ladies', whether it be in teaching a ladies' class, heading up a ladies fellowship or missionary society, handling the nursery schedule (oh, no!), or just having the eyes of the women on every move they make. I know some good ladies who feel that they got more than they bargained for! They had heard that preachers and their wives had to live in glass houses, but no one told them it was *magnifying* glass! Many are confused about how to handle their position in the eyes of the people --- and a few are actually bitter over the dilemma.

The Bible tells us that when the time came for Joshua to assume the leadership of God's chosen people, God explained that He would begin to magnify Joshua in the eyes of the people. I feel that is an important thought to consider. ***"And the Lord said unto Joshua, This day will I begin to magnify thee in the sight of all Israel, that they may know that, as I was with Moses, so I will be with thee."*** *(Joshua 3:7)* ***"On that day the Lord magnified Joshua in the sight of all Israel; and they feared him, as they feared Moses, all the days of his life."*** *(Joshua 4:14)*

94

God magnifies leaders, and makes them bigger than life in the eyes of their followers for evident reasons.

Joshua was promoted from being Moses' servant or apprentice to the primary leadership figure over several million wandering, complaining, faithless children of Israel. (Just take all the complaints and problems of your church members and multiply it several thousand times!) Unlike many of us, Joshua knew what he was getting into; years before the previous generation of Jews were ready to stone him when he encouraged the people to obey God and cross into Canaan. He had watched them for over 40 years as they murmured and complained and rebelled against the Lord under Moses' leadership. Yet he gladly took the leadership when God placed him there because He knew it was the job the Lord had for him to do.

A preacher's wife told me recently about the constant problems and church splits in the church she and her husband had come from as teenagers. She said that throughout their years at Bible college she just kept praying, "Lord, they can't all be like that! There have to be some churches somewhere that don't fight all the time!" They left school and started a church, which to this day has a very sweet and cooperative spirit, yet there have been a few problems through the years where people left the church or turned against the preacher. She related to me how much she cried and agonized over the first people that left, yet I am sure she was much more prepared to expect and accept problems because of the problems she had already seen. Many a lady has been totally devastated by a church split and people's criticism of her husband because she was unprepared and unaware of what those problems would actually be like.

People in the ministry are just that --- people. Yet it's necessary for leaders to be magnified so that people can see

95

clearly and follow. In order for several million Jews to clearly see and follow Joshua, God magnified him, and just as God magnified Joshua in the eyes of the people, he magnifies his preachers today. The preacher's wife who is close to her husband and works closely with him will no doubt live much of her life 'under the magnifying glass,' too, and much of the heartache and hassle she faces will be due to the fact that she is being magnified. I think it helps to stop and realize a few facts about this principle.

UNDER MAGNIFICATION, ALL OBJECTS APPEAR CLOSER THAN THEY ACTUALLY ARE.

Most everyone in the church feels very close to the pastor and his wife. That's good, and probably one of the reasons why the Lord chooses to magnify leadership. However, a problem close up bothers us much more than a problem far away, and a near-by problem we may feel the need (and the qualification) to solve (or complain about) much quicker than a problem far away. The people in our churches, when they see something about us they dislike or disagree with, feel both prompted and justified to let us know. The members need to be close to the preacher and his wife, yet we must realize that this closeness can result in both pleasant and unpleasant feedback, one of those 'occupational hazards' that go with the ministry.

UNDER MAGNIFICATION, ALL OBJECTS AND CHARACTERISTICS APPEAR LARGER THAN THEY ACTUALLY ARE.

Not only do WE appear bigger than we really are, but our strengths and our flaws show up much bigger than reality, as well. Our faults and weaknesses stand out in amazingly graphic detail when people have the opportunity to examine our lives under the magnifying glass. Our strengths and good points often appear much stronger than they are, too (when someone bothers to look for them!) We can't afford to take praise too seriously and allow ourselves to become puffed up and pleased with ourselves. Nor can we allow our critics to discourage and embitter us. We must remember that every characteristic of our lives seems much bigger than it really is, so it's a good idea to take both criticism and praise lightly and with a grain of salt. We are not as good or as bad as most people think!

UNDER MAGNIFICATION, PEOPLE TEND TO SCRUTINIZE AN ISOLATED CHARACTERISTIC RATHER THAN VIEWING THE ENTIRE PICTURE IN PERSPECTIVE.

This is the reason we sometimes feel, "They never notice anything that's good about me, but they certainly can find and critique my weak points!" When you examine a picture or object under a magnifying glass, you don't see the entire picture in its true perspective. You tend rather, to pick out certain points you like or dislike, and to miss seeing how it blends in and contrasts with the rest. It may not make it any easier or more pleasant when people isolate and scrutinize certain areas of our lives, but I think it may help us to realize that this is a natural tendency that comes when the Lord magnifies us in the eyes of others.

I certainly don't consider myself an expert or authority on God's will and work for the preacher's wife, and I sometimes hesitate to share things like this. But I hope that this little thought will be a help to many other preachers' wives as it has been to me. We're privileged and honored to be able to serve the Lord with a good, godly husband, so don't be intimidated about the magnifying glass -- it's all part of the job!

The Preacher's Wife feels sometimes
That her house is made of glass;
"Lord, just a little privacy -
Please, that's all I ask!
There's always someone watching,
They see everything I do,
I'm really getting nervous -
I'd rather hide from just a few!"

But the Lord in loving wisdom
Speaks in understanding tone,
"My precious child, they're watching you,
But you're not all alone.
You walk beside the man who leads,
I've set him before their view,
So naturally, as they follow Him,
They're also watching you."

"My flock has many ladies
Who need example for their life,
So each day they watch intently
The walk of the Preacher's Wife.
You don't need to make them happy --
The One to please is Me,
What's important, while they're watching
Is that I'm pleased with what they see."

"It's My plan for them to watch you,
So don't let it cause you pain;
I magnify My leaders
So the followers' path is plain.
Yes, My child, they're watching,
It's so important what they see -
For while their eyes are on you
They should be clearly seeing Me."

98

Chapter Eleven

I Think I'm Going to Faint!

"Therefore seeing we have this ministry, as we have received mercy, we faint not;" (II Corinthians 4:1)

Have there been times when you felt that you could not go another step, when you felt that you would surely cave in under the burdens that pressed? Spiritual 'fainting fits' have been a universal problem since the beginning of time and have plagued believers of every age. While the word 'faint' has many meanings in Scripture, it always means to lose strength and to fall down on the job. Fainting does not usually take place on the mountain top in times of great victory. We tend to faint in the trials, when discouragement and despair attempt to steal our joy.

It's been said that discouragement is the sin of leaders. It is the tool the devil uses most successfully against people who will not be tempted by alcohol or adultery. The old story is told that the devil held a public sale of all his tools. There were many tools of varying sizes and styles that looked so valuable, yet were priced very cheap. There was one plain wedge, worn from much use, that was labeled, "Not for sale." Someone inquired why the devil would be willing to part with all his other devices, and hang on to one plain old tool like that one.

"That is the most valuable tool I possess," replied the devil. "It is called discouragement. When nothing else will work, I can drive that one lone wedge into a man's heart. Once it has entered I may plant anything there that I desire."

Discouragement is probably the most common cause of spiritual fainting fits, people giving up, throwing in the towel, growing weary of the battle. With it comes the darkness of the soul, the depression and despair that chokes the life out of our service for Christ. Repeatedly the Scriptures warn us against fainting. *"And let us not be weary in well doing: for in due season we shall reap, if we faint not." (Galatians 6:9)*

Charles Spurgeon fought many fierce battles with discouragement and depression, and he penned these words in his book Lectures To My Students in a chapter he titled "The Minister's Fainting Fits." "As it is recorded that David, in the heat of battle, waxed faint, so may it be written of all the servants of the Lord. Fits of depression come over the most of us. Usually cheerful as we may be, we must at intervals be cast down. The strong are not always vigorous, the wise not always ready, the brave not always courageous, and the joyous not always happy. There may be here and there men of iron, to whom wear and tear work no perceptible detriment, but surely the rust frets even these; and as for ordinary men, the Lord knows, and makes them to know, that they are but dust."

"Knowing by most painful experience what deep depression of spirit means, being visited therewith at seasons by no means few or far between, I thought it might be consolatory to some of my brethren if I gave my thoughts thereon, that younger men might not fancy that some strange thing had happened to them when they became for a season possessed by melancholy; and that sadder men might know that one upon whom the sun has shone right joyously did not always walk in the light. It is not necessary by quotations from the biographies of eminent ministers to prove that seasons of fearful prostration have fallen to the lot of most, if not all of them. The life of Luther might suffice to give a thousand instances, and he was by no means of the weaker sort."

The word 'faint' is translated from several different Greek and Hebrew words, and carries several connotations. It means to toil to the point of intense weariness, to show one's feebleness, to wrap oneself in self-pity, to turn out badly, to cave in, to loosen or relax in the conflict. Sometimes fainting is the result of emotional and spiritual distress. Often it is the by-product of physical exhaustion. At times it is a bitter result of responding incorrectly to the Lord's dealing in our lives. More often than not, it is the natural weariness that results from fighting a long conflict. Yet we are warned in every instance not to faint. *"Men ought always to pray and not to faint." (Luke 18:1)*

One of the vulnerable times for fainting is when it is necessary for the Lord to use the chastening rod in our lives. Scripture admonishes us, *"...Despise not thou the chastening of the Lord, nor faint when thou art rebuked of him: For whom the Lord loveth he chasteneth, and scourgeth every son whom he receiveth." (Hebrews 12:5-6)* We must be very careful when the Lord deals with our hearts that we respond correctly to His chastening. There is sometimes a temptation to react in bitterness, or to give up in despair, but the correct response to chastening is confession and submission. An old New England Primer carried the lines, "Job feels the Rod Yet blesses God." May we also learn to respond correctly to the chastening hand of our loving Father and not faint when He must rebuke us.

Someone said that, "Courage is not in having the strength to go on, but in going on when you don't have the strength." If we lose hope and give in to despair, fainting is inevitable. David said, *"I had fainted, unless I had believed to see the goodness of the Lord in the land of the living."* *(Psalm 27:13)* Without faith that the ultimate victory is secure, we will falter and faint in the midst of the battle.

When we face trials and testings day after day, it is easy to get the "oh-poor-me's" and fall into the Slough of Despond. One of the translations of the word faint actually means 'to wrap oneself in self-pity.' Feeling sorry for ourselves never makes the load any lighter, but always brings on fainting. Unless we keep our eyes on Christ we will succumb to despondency's vice-like grip. *"For consider him that endured such contradiction of sinners against himself, lest ye be wearied and faint in your minds."* *(Hebrews 12:3)*

Often fainting in our spiritual lives is a direct result of the over-taxing of our physical bodies. Such was a major contributor in Elijah's bout with despondency under the juniper tree. He had just experienced his greatest victory. He had gone without physical nourishment. He had run a long distance and taxed his physical strength to the very limit. No wonder he found himself in a state of helpless despair, wondering what was wrong with him!

Jonah succumbed to fainting twice during the part of his ministry we find recorded. When he had fled from the command of God and met God's chastening rod, he found himself in the belly of the whale despairing of his very life. *"When my soul fainted within me I remembered the Lord: and my prayer came in unto thee, into thine holy temple."*

102

(Jonah 2:7) The word that is translated 'fainted' here is the word *ataph* which means 'to show oneself feeble'. In this instance, when Jonah fainted, he realized and admitted his own inability to rescue himself. His response to fainting was humility toward God, and the Lord responded by speaking to the fish, and the fish vomited Jonah out on dry land. God began to use Jonah again in His service.

In chapter four we find Jonah backslidden again, this time in angry bitterness against God because He had mercy upon the Ninevites and did not destroy them as Jonah had prophesied. *"And it came to pass, when the sun did arise, that God prepared a vehement east wind; and the sun beat upon the head of Jonah, that he fainted, and wished himself to die, and said, It is better for me to die than to live."* *(Jonah 4:8)* In this instance, *alaph* is the word used for 'fainted,' which means 'to cover or wrap oneself up.' This instance of fainting was different in that Jonah responded to God in self-pity and anger and bitterness. We never read of Jonah being used of God again.

The Apostle Paul faced much more distress and pressure than most of us encounter in our daily lives. He reminds us often of the perils he faced and the oppositions he encountered, yet he never quit, he never despaired of the victory, and he never broke under the strain.

In the fourth chapter of II Corinthians, Paul shares with us the keys that kept him from fainting. In verse one, he says that he had his eyes on the ministry of reaching the lost with the Gospel. *"Therefore seeing we have this ministry, as we have received mercy, we faint not."* He couldn't quit or give up because of the many people that would die and go to Hell without the Gospel. He said that he could resist fainting in his ministry in the same measure that he had received mercy -- without limit.

In verse 7 he reminds us that we have this glorious

treasure contained in 'earthen vessels,' finite, weak bodies and minds that often bend beneath the strain. *"But we have this treasure in earthen vessels, that the excellency of the power may be of God, and not of us."* When we realize our own weakness and inability, we can sincerely give God all the glory for what is accomplished through our lives.

He also realized that the troubles and heartaches that come into our lives are not because of God's lack of love toward us, but to fashion and mold our lives according to the likeness of Christ. *"For we which live are alway delivered unto death for Jesus' sake, that the life also of Jesus might be made manifest in our mortal flesh."* (*verse 11*) It is God's great love for us, and His desire for our lives to glorify Him, that allows problems and heartaches to come into our lives.

"For all things are for your sakes, that the abundant grace might through the thanksgiving of many redound to the glory of God." (*verse 15*) This verse seems to echo the assurance found in Romans 8:28. *"And we know that all things work together for good to them that love God, to them who are the called according to his purpose."* Very often we must rely on that assurance when we cannot understand the why's and how's of what God chooses for us. "God sometimes conceals His purposes so that we will be consoled by His promises."

Paul concludes his lesson on "How Not To Faint" by saying, *"For which cause* (because I know that everything God allows is best for me and will cause me to become more Christ-like and bring glory to the Lord) *we faint not; but though our outward man perish, yet the inward man is renewed day by day. For our light affliction, which is but for a moment, worketh for us a far more exceeding and eternal weight of glory; While we look not at the things which are seen, but at the things which are not seen: for the things which are seen are temporal; but the things which are not seen are eternal." (verses 16-18)*

Regardless of the outward circumstances, I must come to the Holy Spirit daily for a fresh 'renewing of my mind' (Romans 12:2), and as a Spirit-filled individual have my eyes on God's eternal purposes rather than my own temporary problems. Again his advice is reminiscent of Romans 8:28, where he concludes: *"For I reckon that the sufferings of this present time are not worthy to be compared with the glory which shall be revealed in us." (Romans 8:18)*

No matter what the causes are in our individual lives, fainting is a perilous danger to our spiritual well-being. The fainting itself is usually recovered from easily, but irreparable damage may be inflicted in the fall. Jonah's second fainting fit was evidently a fatal one.

I'm sure the devil is not any nicer to you than he is to me. Every day there are a hundred new reasons to quit -- to go to pieces -- to say, "I just can't take it anymore." And that's exactly what he would like to see us do. But I need to say, "As I have obtained mercy, I faint not." What is the limit on the mercy that God has lovingly extended to me? There is no limit. What was the limit God placed on how much he would pay to rescue my soul? He gave His all, His very Son, and promised to *'with him freely give us all things.'*

How can I place a limit on what I am willing to do, how far I'm willing to go, what price I am willing to pay? I can say, "In the same measure I have obtained mercy, will I go on for God and obey His command to 'faint not'." No matter what the devil throws at me, no matter what the Lord allows to test me or to mold me, I won't give up, I won't give in, I won't give out -- I'll just go on and give it my best.

And you and I can both go on in if we learn to 'collect'

on the promise of Isaiah 40:31. *"But they that wait upon the Lord shall renew their strength, they shall mount up with wings as eagles; they shall run and not be weary, they shall walk and not faint."*

Chapter Twelve

A Difference of Perspective

*"And they told him...We came unto the land whither thou
sentest us, and surely it floweth with milk and honey;
and this is the fruit of it...And Caleb stilled the people
before Moses, and said, Let us go up at once, and possess
it; for we are well able to overcome it. But the men that
went up with him said, We be not able to go up against
the people; for they are stronger than we."*
(Numbers 13:27, 30-31)

Problems! Problems! Problems! Everybody has them.
It has occurred to me that the victorious Christians have
them just like the defeated Christians do. What makes the
difference in how the problems turn out, and how their lives
progress? One man summed it up in saying, "It all depends
on how you look at it. Don't look at the Lord through your
circumstances, look at your circumstances through the
Lord." While some folks have their eyes on their problems,
others have their eyes on God's promises. It all adds up to
A Difference Of Perspective.

Our story in Numbers is a prime example of how important it is that we face life's problems correctly. Moses and the children of Israel certainly had their share of problems and difficulties, and with three and a half million people together, I'm sure the problems mounted up enormously.

A man who had been a general in the U. S. Army released the following figures. It would have taken 1,500 tons of food every day just to keep the Israelites from starving to death, and to feed them the way that we eat would take 4,000 tons of food a day. If they only had enough water to drink and wash a few dishes, it would take 11 million gallons every single day. This could fill a freight train of tank cars 1,800 miles long! To set up camp for one night would necessitate 750 square miles, two-thirds the size of the State of Rhode Island. They had been trapped between Pharoah's mighty army and the Red Sea. They had received their water from a rock and their food from the sky. Again and again they had faced insurmountable odds that the Lord had easily overcome. You would think that they would begin to learn to trust in Him.

Now they came to the real test, and sadly failed. All the earlier 'quizzes' had just been in preparation for the 'final exam,' and yet they had missed the lessons God meant for them to learn. Just as Esther had come to the throne 'for such a time as this,' the nation Israel came to their most important event to date and blew it. Now it was time for them to cross over the Jordan River that separated between them and the land of promise, the perfect will of God. But again they measured the battles against their own capabilities rather than God's. They could see the problems clearly, but the promises had become obscure.

"And they brought up an evil report of the land which they had searched unto the children of Israel, saying, The

land, through which we have gone to search it, is a land that eateth up the inhabitants thereof; and all the people that we saw in it are men of a great stature. And there we saw the giants...and we were in our own sight as grasshoppers..." (Numbers 13:32-33) Ten out of twelve had their eyes on the problems.

But for every problem there must be a promise. The children of Israel had many promises. *"And the Lord said, I have surely seen the affliction of my people... And I am come down to deliver them out of the hand of the Egyptians, and to bring them up out of that land unto a land flowing with milk and honey;" (Exodus 3:7-8)* God had miraculously fulfilled the first part of this promise, yet the people were slow to believe that He could as easily finish this task and give them the land of Canaan.

After all the prayers that the Lord has answered and all the promises that He has kept in our lives, we can still find ourselves doubting if we stop to evaluate the situation by our own abilities and resources. Israel got into deep trouble because they were seeking to find out IF they could do what God had commanded them, rather than looking to see HOW to do what God said. Anytime we give ourselves an option of whether or not to obey God, we will stumble.

Only two men of the 12 believed God could and would keep His Word. Caleb and Joshua pleaded with the people, *"Only rebel not ye against the Lord, neither fear ye the people of the land: for they are bread for us: their defence is departed from them, and the Lord is with us: fear them not." (Numbers 14:9)* Disobedience always demands a high price, and it cost the children of Israel the remainder of their lives. All of the adults were sentenced to live out their days wandering in the wilderness, and only Joshua and Caleb were permitted to enter into the Promised Land with the next generation. All of this because they failed to see

109

the promises and looked only at the problems.

The Bible Hall Of Faith is decorated with the memories of many who believed the promises in spite of the problems that they faced. Abraham rested his entire hope in the promise of a son, in spite of the fact that he and Sarah were childless and up in years. Noah believed God's promise of deliverance from a watery judgment in spite of the fact that rain had never yet been seen. *"These all died in faith, not having received the promises, but having seen them afar off, and were persuaded of them, and embraced them, and confessed that they were strangers and pilgrims on the earth."* *(Hebrews 11:13)* Some of them never got to see the complete fulfillment of the promise that God made, and yet never lost faith that God could bring it to pass.

Dr. Adoniram Judson laboured diligently for six years in Burma before he baptized one convert. At the end of three years of seemingly unrewarded hard work, he was asked what evidence he had of ultimate success. Judson replied, "As much as there is a God who will fulfill all His promises." A hundred churches and thousands of converts were the answer to his unwavering faith.

At one point in Bunyan's allegory, *Pilgrim's Progress*, Christian decides to leave the Main Highway to follow an easier path, but it leads him into the territory of Giant Despair's Doubting Castle. Eventually, Christian is captured by Giant Despair and kept in a dungeon. He is advised to kill himself and for a time it seems that Christian has been totally conquered by Despair. But Hope reminds him of previous victories and they begin to pray. Christian soon comes to this realization: "What a fool am I thus to lie in this stinking dungeon, when I may as well be at liberty. I have a Key in my bosom called Promise that will, I am persuaded, open any lock in Doubting Castle." Hope encouraged him, "That's good news, Brother, pluck it out of thy bosom and try." The key of Promise easily turned the great lock, and the prison gates flew open, freeing Christian from Despair.

Promises can also be vital keys in our own lives to release us from the seemingly hopeless situations we sometimes face. But God's promises left unappropriated are like checks left uncashed -- worth no more than the paper they are printed on. Why should we live in spiritual poverty and famine when we have God's best blessings offered us freely in His Word? *"But my God shall supply all your needs according to his riches in glory by Christ Jesus." (Philippians 4:19) "But seek ye first the kingdom of God, and his righteousness, and all these things shall be added unto you." (Matthew 6:33)*

Our lives are hanging in the balance, and how we face life's problems will be a vital determining factor in the direction our lives will go. The problems often loom large in our pathway, especially when we try to look at all the problems that we might encounter during the next year, instead of just the problems that actually are upon us today.

It was a wise Christian who first prayed, "Lord help me to remember that nothing is going to happen to me today that You and I together cannot handle." The future is as bright as the promises of God, and His promises are many and mighty. There is a promise for every day, for every need, for every life. We simply need to claim them in prayer and obedience and see God work miracles in our lives.

Do we view our problems in light of God's promises? Or do we see God's promises faintly through our problems? Our response, right or wrong, may well decide the course our lives take, as it did for this entire generation of disobedient Israelites. Let's not live our lives wandering in the wilderness of sin when we could be enjoying the milk

111

and honey of God's perfect will for our lives.

In many of the trying circumstances that we face, the only difference between victory and defeat is A DIFFERENCE OF PERSPECTIVE.

Chapter Thirteen

When Good Girls Go Bad

"That they may teach the young women to be sober, to love their husbands, to love their children, To be discreet, chaste, keepers at home, good, obedient to their own husbands, that the word of God be not blasphemed."
(Titus 2:4-5)

A solemn warning is issued to the feminine population in our text verse, a statement that always causes me to pause and ponder as I read through the book of Titus. A descriptive listing is given of the qualities that should characterize the lives of Christian young women, covering their attitudes, actions, and aspirations. Thoughtful judgments, proper family relationships, discretion, chastity, homemaking skills and goals, and submission are all included.

The timely views concerning women in the 1990's are in sharp contrast to these timeless Scriptural ideals, even in many of our churches. As ladies who belong to Christ, it is imperative that we take a close look at the exhortations and examples contained in the Bible. The import of our conduct is stressed in the latter portion of the verse, *"...that the word of God be not blasphemed."*

The important things for us to learn are not fashion do's and don'ts, career guidelines, and how to compete for equality with the male populace. The things we are to be learning are on the opposite pole from the knowledge that most ladies are seeking. If we were studying for a degree in Feminine Godliness, some of the required courses would be those outlined in this passage:

HUSBAND-LOVING: The Bible lists this along with other important characteristics that are to be learned. So 'falling in love' is not enough, we must also 'learn' to love our husbands, as love is 'willfully choosing to do what is best for another, regardless of personal expense.' *philandros* Literally means 'lover of husband.' Denotes tender affection.

CHILDREN-LOVING: Again, love means 'to do what is best for another, regardless of personal expense'. Loving our children means training them, providing for their needs, disciplining or 'discipling' them, as well as demonstrating our love to them physically and verbally. *philoteknos* Literally means 'lover of children,' again denotes tender affection.

DISCRETION: Soundness of mind, propriety, good taste, especially concerning our conduct toward men. *"As a jewel of gold in a swine's snout, so is a fair woman which is without discretion."* *(Proverbs 11:22)* The words 'sober' and 'discreet' in this passage are closely related, *sophron* and *sophronizo*. The root literally means 'to save the mind.'

114

Sober-minded, temperate, of good judgment.

CHASTITY: Purity of mind, body, heart, and character. The root word *hagnos* speaks of being consecrated, set apart, or saved for a specific purpose. Especially indicates a woman or girl keeping herself for her husband only. Paul uses this to illustrate our relationship to Christ. *"For I am jealous over you with godly jealousy: for I have espoused you to one husband, that I may present you as a chaste virgin to Christ."* *(2 Corinthians 11:2)* Modest, immaculate, pure from fault, pure from carnality.

HOMEMAKING: The job of a wife and mother is more than just housekeeping -- it is homemaking. In order to make a house a home, a woman must use a little bit of creativity and a whole lot of love. It's been said many times, "While houses are built of brick and stone, homes are made of love alone."

> The beauty of a house is harmony.
> The security of a house is loyalty.
> The joy of a house is love.
> The plenty of a house is children.
> The rule of a house is service.
> The comfort of a house is God Himself.

Oikouros, the word translated 'keepers at home,' means one who works at home, one who keeps her own house. Indicates that home is her work-place and that her work centers around her home. This is exemplified in detail by the Virtuous Woman of Proverbs 31. *"She looketh well to the ways of her household, and eateth not the bread of idleness."* *(Proverbs 31:27)*

115

GOODNESS: Morally honorable, good in character and constitution, beneficial in effect. *Agathos.* Good not only in what you do, but in what you are. *"Even so every good tree bringeth forth good fruit; but a corrupt tree bringeth forth evil fruit...Wherefore by their fruits ye shall know them."* *(Matthew 7:18, 20)*

SUBMISSION: *"...to be obedient unto their own husbands..."* *hupotasso* Literally, 'to hear - under,' to listen and submit to God-ordained authority. *"Wives, submit yourselves unto your own husbands, as unto the Lord... Therefore as the church is subject unto Christ, so let the wives be to their own husbands in every thing."* *(Ephesians 5:22-24)*

How important are these traits in our lives? *"..that the word of God be not blasphemed"* sounds pretty serious. The first time I realized the weight of those words I was shocked that I could blaspheme God's word, not only with my mouth, but also with my life. The word *blasphemeo* means 'to blaspheme, rail at, to speak injuriously.'

Ladies, what does the world think of the Word of God as they see it interpreted through our works and words every day? Sin is a crime in the eyes of God for anyone, but when the world knows that we belong to Christ and then we willfully disobey God's word, we bring shame upon Christ and do serious damage to the work of God.

Today, more than ever before, women who once lived right are departing from their rightful place in the home and from God's righteous standards. There is more adultery and promiscuity among church people, more immodest and improper dress among Christian women, and more indiscretion than ever in the history of the church. Real spirituality is sadly lacking in the lives of women. How

116

desperately we need to understand the effect of our testimony upon the work of God. *"Sin is a reproach to any people"* -- but especially so when it takes place among the people of God.

Dinah was a girl who must have minimized the importance of her personal testimony. While she was one of God's chosen people and partaker of the blessings and leadership that God provided to Jacob's family, she must have considered herself 'part of the group' rather than personally responsible to God. In Genesis 34, Dinah evidently had become bored with the life God had chosen for herself and her family, and decided to go see what other girls did instead. *"And Dinah... went out to see the daughters of the land. And when Shechem... saw her, he took her, and lay with her, and defiled her."* (Genesis 34:1-2) Her interest in worldliness cost Dinah her virtue.

Although Dinah was disgraced, she was not the only one injured in the tragedy. No one goes down alone -- everyone who sins hurts others as well as himself. Dinah brought grief upon her entire family, and the result of her sin prompted her brothers to sin. They deceived the men of Shechem in promising to intermarry with their people if they would be circumcised. The men agreed, and while they were still sore from the procedure, Simeon and Levi slew all the men of the city, and the brothers took the women and children captive and spoiled the houses.

"And Jacob said to Simeon and Levi, Ye have troubled me to make me to stink among the inhabitants of the land..." (Genesis 34:30) The same people who had once respected Jacob's family and revered God because of their testimony now scorned them and mocked God, and Jacob's family had to move away. The testimony of the whole family was a stench in the nostrils of the world. When Dinah went out to see the daughters of the land she had no

intention of bringing so much heartache upon herself, her family, and her God. Sin always has a hidden price tag, and the costs are far greater than we can afford.

David was another Christian whose sin brought reproach upon the name of God. David had been known as *'a man after God's own heart,'* and had led the entire nation in service and worship to God. Then David chose his physical passions above his spiritual desires, and committed adultery with Bathsheba. Before the ordeal was ended, David had also lied, gotten a man drunk, and killed him in order to hide the sin. David ended up losing three sons for the one man that was killed, and his family was plagued with heartache throughout the rest of David's lifetime. Nathan, the prophet, exposed David's sin and told him, *"...by this deed thou hast given great occasion to the enemies of the Lord to blaspheme..." (2 Samuel 12:13)*

When God's people indulge in sin, it always takes them deeper into the mire than they ever dreamed they could go, and always brings reproach upon Christianity before the world. When people who have been deep in sin repent and do great things for Him, it brings God much glory. When those who have been living for God turn back to sin and worldliness, it brings Him great reproach.

It is important that ladies realize the weighty importance of their actions, and the effect that their testimony has upon the Word of God. *"That the word of God be not blasphemed"* is a mighty important reason for us to avoid the shame and reproach that comes WHEN GOOD GIRLS GO BAD.

Chapter Fourteen

Getting Safely Around Life's Stumblingblocks

"But whoso shall offend one of these little ones which believe in me, it were better for him that a millstone were hanged about his neck, and that he were drowned in the depth of the sea. Woe unto the world because of offences! for it must needs be that offences come: but woe to that man by whom the offence cometh!"
(Matthew 18:6-7)

Two plus two equals four. What goes up must come down. Sooner or later someone will hurt you or disappoint you. There are facts of life that you cannot change -- so you must learn to deal with them. Our text verse assures us that stumblingblocks will come, but woe unto that one that causes God's children to stumble.

Stumblingblocks are just a fact of life. Every person WILL encounter stumblingblocks, a person or event that *could* cause you to stumble in your Christian life. It may be a person that you know, or maybe just someone you know of, their actions, their poor testimony, their hidden sin that is suddenly revealed. It could be the greatest shock of your life. It may be linked to an event that brings great disappointment. It might be something that hurts you deeper than you think you can stand.

But I'm here to tell you that you CAN stand. You CAN deal with your hurt and disappointment. You CAN learn from it. You CAN be better, not bitter, because of it. You can keep going, keep growing, and keep serving the Lord no matter what someone else has done. If you don't need this little piece of encouragement and instruction right now, please keep reading, because someday every one of us will face one of life's stumblingblocks. I'm here to post a warning that says, "Watch your step! Beware of fallen stumblingblocks up ahead!" I want to do all I can to protect you from that sudden fall.

It may be the person you look up to the most, the one that you have learned from and followed all through your Christian life. You might have considered this person to be the greatest Christian you've ever known. But it's not always someone whom you consider to be above you in authority, in Christian maturity, and in example and teaching.

It could be someone that you've loved and cared for and patiently taught and rejoiced as they grew and learned and became more Christlike. It may be your most fruitful convert or even your very own child. I don't know who it is in your life that will become a stumblingblock, but I know that there will be some.

Consider in your mind for a moment what might cause a person to stumble. You're walking along, unaware of any dangerous obstacles, one foot in front of the other. Maybe you're preoccupied about something. Maybe you're carrying a big load in your arms, and can't see clearly what's coming up ahead. Maybe you're weak, faint, or dazed from something that has already happened to you. Suddenly you trip over something you didn't know was ahead and before you realize what has happened, you have already taken a fall.

How bad will you be hurt? It could be a minor bruise. It could be fatal. It could be anything in between. That all depends on how far you fall and the position you're in when you land. You will face a stumblingblock up ahead. Since you don't know how badly you might be injured if you stumble, your best protection is to keep from stumbling over them.

1. Expect Stumblingblocks.

Our best protection is to be looking for them. I don't mean being on a witch-hunt, or being skeptical and cynical about every Christian and every preacher that you know. I just mean being realistic. People are human. People fail. If you keep that in mind, it won't be as likely to knock the wind out of you. There is a stumblingblock somewhere up ahead. You'll trip over it if you don't see it. You won't see it if you're not watching for it. The time to prevent a nasty fall is before you stumble.

"It shouldn't happen." No, but it will. No one should leave a deadly knife laying around in a dangerous place. But if someone does, it doesn't automatically mean you must be wounded by it. You can learn to recognize and deal with the danger, and come out BETTER for the experience. You don't have to let it destroy you.

The Bible says that a saved person falling before the unsaved is a corrupt spring; it can poison you if you let it.

121

"A righteous man falling down before the wicked is as a troubled fountain, and a corrupt spring." *(Proverbs 25:26)* But if there's a sign posted beside the well that says, "Danger! Contaminated Water! Do Not Drink!" then it's my own fault if I allow it to poison me. Proverbs 22:3 gives this advice: *"A prudent man foreseeth the evil, and hideth himself: but the simple pass on, and are punished."* If you're wise, you'll see the danger ahead and protect yourself and others from falling over a stumblingblock.

Some years ago, a person fell into sin and wrecked their ministry. One young lady told me, "So and so sinned and I was hurt by it. Now I don't believe any preachers are for real, so I don't feel any responsibility to obey what they preach. I was hurt by that person's actions, and that's why I'm not doing right." In later years she was guilty of the same sin that he had committed.

Another young lady told me, "I was terribly disappointed by what he did. But there was a time when he served God with all his heart. One sermon that he preached was used by God to turn my life around. While I wish he were still pure and serving the Lord, that doesn't undo how the Lord used him in the past. That sermon's principles are still an important part of my life." The same stumblingblock, but far different responses, that resulted in different endings to their stories.

2. Walk in the Light.

In order to avoid tripping on a stumblingblock, you must be able to see it. Walk in light all the time, and you'll be more likely to see them before you've fallen. Be Bible-Centered. *"Thy word is a lamp unto my feet, and a light unto my path."* *(Psalm 119:105)* If you keep the light of God's Word shining brightly on your path at all times, it will protect you from the stumblingblocks.

"Great peace have they which love thy law, and nothing shall offend them." *(Psalm 119:165)* One of the definitions of the word 'offend' in Cruden's Concordance is 'to be scandalized, or made to stumble by the example of another.' If you love the Bible, and let it become an integral part of your life and your thinking, it will protect you. Everyone will be hurt sometime in their lives, but it doesn't have to destroy you. Get in the Bible. Stay in the Bible. Memorize it. Read it. Meditate on it. Let it become a part of you.

3. Let People be Human.

Don't get caught up in man worship. The best preacher or Christian leader in all the world is still human flesh and blood, still a saved sinner, still vulnerable to sin and temptation. *"For all flesh is as grass, and all the glory of man as the flower of grass. The grass withereth and the flower thereof falleth away: But the word of the Lord endureth for ever. And this is the word which by the gospel is preached unto you."* *(I Peter 1 :24-25)* All men are fallible; only the Bible that they preach is not.

God has given us leaders in His plan. He wants us to follow their leadership. He does not want them to become the God we serve. We should love them, serve with them, pray for them, and do all we can to support them as they follow God. But we should never lose sight of the fact that they are human.

In Joshua 3:7 I learned something about leaders. *"And the Lord said unto Joshua, This day will I begin to magnify thee in the sight of all Israel, that they may know that, as I was with Moses, so I will be with thee."* God chose to magnify leaders. It's part of His plan. God has

123

good reasons for doing so. Magnification makes an object look bigger, clearer, and closer than it will look without magnification. God wants us to see our leaders that way. But when you magnify an object, it doesn't actually make it any bigger -- it just looks bigger. Those leaders that God has magnified in our view are just normal people who are serving God, and because of their faithfulness God has chosen to put His magnifying glass on them, so that they stand out from the crowd.

First Corinthians 11:1 is where Paul gives us some good advice about following the leadership of a man of God. *"Be ye followers of me, even as I also am of Christ."* Look to the leader, but don't stop there. Look beyond the leader to Christ. When a leader steps out of line and is no longer following Christ, you keep following the Lord. Don't go off in the direction that man or woman has gone. Don't go off in your own wrong direction in self-pity. Just keep following Christ and His Word and His will for your life. Paul didn't say, "Be ye followers of me," and stop there. He put this condition on it, "...as I also am of Christ." He only wanted them to follow him as long as he followed the Lord.

Man-worship puts you off balance. You get to leaning too far in some man's direction, and you'll be in a precarious position. Being off balance just means it will take less force for the devil to knock you off your feet. But you keep drawing closer to God, and you will be standing tall with your feet planted firmly on the ground. You'll be much less apt to take a fall.

There ARE some preachers and Christians who will disappoint you. *"For the priest's lips should keep knowledge, and they should seek the law at his mouth: for he is the messenger of the Lord of hosts. But ye are departed out of the way; ye have caused many to stumble at the law; ye have corrupted the covenant of Levi, saith*

124

the Lord of hosts." (Malachi 2:7-8) There have been some people in the Gospel ministry who weren't for real, and misused God's church and God's people. But they are few, thank the Lord, and God can expose them for what they are.

There have been many others who 'did run well,' but got side-tracked in sin and hurt those that they had loved and never dreamed they'd ever hurt. That's who the devil is after, and he is relentless in his efforts to cause real men and women of God to fall into sin, and become a stumblingblock that will cause others to fall. I truly believe that the devil works harder to destroy the lives and homes of preachers and their wives than anyone else on earth. I've seen a lot of havoc that he has created. It's not just bad people who wreck their lives. There are some good people who got off-track somewhere along the line. It might not have come to light immediately, but sooner or later those chickens come home to roost.

Pray for your preacher. Pray for each other. We're all in need of God's strength and God's armor in order to stand against the attacks of Satan.

4. Differentiate between People and the Lord.

"So and so hurt me so I'm just going to quit!" When you got saved who did you receive into your heart? Has the Lord ever let you down or hurt you or disappointed you? Tell me, why would you sin against God because of what a person has done to hurt you. God didn't hurt you, did He?

Someone told me that several years ago. "This thing happened and I just quit. I'm not going to take any more of this." I said, "Is that the person you were serving and living for? Is that who saved you from hell?" Why are we so dumb? Don't blame God for what God didn't do. If you are serving the Lord, make up your mind that you'll never

125

quit because of a person. I didn't start because of them. I'm not going to stop because of them.

You do need to realize that when you're hurt, you're in danger of making impulsive wrong decisions that haven't been thought through and have no rational basis. Don't make decisions when you're hurting. Don't quit what you're doing. Don't start doing something else. Just keep on keeping on and give yourself time to recover from the wounds that you've received. God will bless you for your faithfulness, and He will reward you for it.

5. Keep a Balanced Attitude.

There are two sides to every coin, and there is a balancing that we need to do in our attitude concerning people who are stumblingblocks. Side one -- Remember that when someone has preached the Gospel and then sins, the good they have done in preaching, teaching, soulwinning, serving, exhorting, and comforting does not excuse their wrong. "But they're winning souls." That doesn't justify dishonesty and theft and adultery. "But he's a great preacher." Not unless he's at least trying to live what he preaches. "They were there for me when I needed them." Don't ever forget how God used them to be a blessing to you in the past, but that doesn't justify sin. The right that he preached did not justify the wrong that he practiced.

Flip side -- Neither does their wrongdoing nullify the truth they once preached. God's Word is still true and powerful and it's principles of right and wrong are still the same. Don't just throw away all the good things that God used that person to preach or accomplish if they line up with Bible. I know of a pastor in a southern state who once lived and preached the same convictions and standards that we have. But he felt that he was done wrong by the man who first taught him those convictions. So when he threw that friendship out the window, with it he threw out every conviction he had ever preached.

That makes me wonder if the man ever really had any convictions of his own, or if he was just mimicking what he heard somewhere else. You need to establish your own convictions. Don't ignore the preaching, but find out why the preacher says that and believes that. Study it in the Bible and settle it for yourself. If your standards don't become your own, they will be the first thing to go overboard in a storm.

The right that he preached doesn't justify the wrong that he did. That wrong that he did doesn't nullify the right that he preached. Though all flesh is as grass, *"the word of God liveth and abideth forever."*

6. Guard your Heart.

Proverbs 4:23 says *"Keep thy heart with all diligence, for out of it are the issues of life."* If there's ever a time you need to put some extra emphasis on guarding your heart, it's when you face a stumblingblock. Don't become bitter. Don't become cynical. Don't become suspicious of everybody and everything. Don't become judgmental. "If that's what Christianity is, then I don't want any part of it." How many times have you heard those kinds of statements before?

Don't write off God and the Bible based on one act of a mere mortal. Don't even write off that person's whole life. Good people fall into sin. Good people get backslidden. That's who the devil is working the hardest on. Most of all, don't stereotype all Christians or all preachers into one category. Let each person rise or fall on their own merit.

127

Don't suspect everyone of what one person did.

7. DON'T QUIT!

Even if you can't keep from being knocked down, don't be knocked out. Don't be devastated by it. When someone hurts or disappoints you, don't let the devil tell you that you can't cope with it and learn from it. *"There hath no temptation taken you but such as is common to man: but God is faithful, who will not suffer you to be tempted above that ye are able; but will with the temptation also make a way to escape, that ye may be able to bear it."*

I heard a touching illustration of that verse, likening God to a pharmacist who carefully mixed medicine into capsules, watchful to put in just the right dosage so that it will not harm the person that it is meant to help. God wants to use this experience in your life. He is able to make all things work together for good in your life. He is very careful not to give you more than you can bear. You can do it!

7. Don't Let it Make a Stumblingblock out of You.

Just because that person becomes a stumblingblock to you, doesn't mean you have to become a stumblingblock to others who love you and look to you. Don't face God at the Judgment with a destroyed life based on someone else's Christianity or lack of it. "If a hypocrite is what stands between you and God, it just means that he's closer to God than you are." There's some truth to that statement.

"Let us therefore follow after the things which make for peace, and things wherewith one may edify another...It is good neither to eat flesh, nor to drink wine, nor any thing whereby thy brother stumbleth, or is offended, or is

128

made weak." *(Romans 14:19,21)* Be careful after you have faced a stumblingblock, that you don't become one in the path of someone else. If you quit, you'll cause someone else to stumble. If you get bitter, you'll cause someone to stumble. If you use this as an excuse to do wrong, you'll cause someone to stumble. It might be someone that you love very much and would never want to hurt. Instead, become an edifier, a builder, and a strengthener. Follow after that which edifies and builds and strengthens.

I hope that this will be the encouragement you need to get through this tough spot in your life, whether you face a stumblingblock today, or it still waits in the future. There are stumblingblocks up ahead, but you don't have to fall. You don't have to let it destroy your life. You can protect yourself from a fatal fall at one of life's stumblingblocks, and walk carefully around them 'considering thyself, lest thou also be tempted.' You can also post the warning sign for someone else.

"And I thank
Christ Jesus
our Lord,
who hath enabled me,
for that he
counted me faithful,
putting me into
the ministry;"
I Timothy 1:12

Chapter Fifteen

What To Do When You Don't Know What To Do

"O our God, wilt thou not judge them? for we have no might against this great company that cometh against us: neither know we what to do; but our eyes are upon thee."
(II Chronicles 20:12)

I want to share with you one simple truth that is not all that exciting or dynamic, that you probably already know, but that I need to be reminded of again. What do you do when you don't know what to do? Where do you turn when there's no one to turn to? What do you say when you're lost for words, or the lump in your throat prohibits speaking? There are occasions in every lifetime that find us suddenly between a rock and a hard place, when every option looks like the worst one possible. It is what we do in these times

131

that reveals much about what we really are, and it is what we do in these times that determines to some extent where we are and what we do in the good times. If we could just hang on to this one truth, it would save us many tragic mistakes made in the heat of a situation. What should you do when you don't know what to do? Just keep your eyes on the Lord!

In II Chronicles 20, we read of King Jehoshaphat being told that the Moabites and the Ammonites had allied themselves and were on their way to attack King Jehoshaphat's army in Judah. Jehoshaphat had just returned and repented of what was probably the most serious error he had made in all of his reign. He had yoked himself and the forces of Judah with ungodly Ahab, against the counsel of God's prophet, Micaiah. He was mistaken for Ahab, which nearly cost him his life, yet when he cried out to the Lord in the midst of the battle he was miraculously delivered.

Now he suddenly met with a new and greater danger; it is quite possible that the army of Judah was not yet recovered from the losses sustained at Ramoth-gilead, and they were helpless in the face of this new attack. Jehoshaphat was definitely in the midst of an emergency. He readily admitted, *"...neither know we what to do."* And yet he was to see a miracle take place in his behalf, and the power of God come to his rescue. Surely we could learn what he did in a crisis, to aid us in the situations we encounter that present the question: What Do You Do When You Don't Know What To Do?

The first thing that Jehoshaphat did was to pray. Before running off to call the troops to order, or doing anything in his own human strength, he, himself, began to seek the Lord's help. *"And Jehoshaphat feared, and set himself to seek the LORD..."* *(II Chronicles 20:4)* After he began himself to seek the Lord's help, he led the people to petition the Lord with him. *"...and proclaimed a fast throughout all Judah. And Judah gathered themselves together, to ask help of the Lord: even out of all the cities of Judah they came to seek the LORD."* I fear that many times leadership challenges the people to pray about a need, when they have not yet begun to pray themselves. Still other leaders pray alone, and never challenge the people they lead to join them in the supplication. This account teaches us that the leader who first prayed himself, and then challenged the people to pray with him, saw the mighty hand of God intervene.

When they began to pray, the first theme of their prayer was the omnipotence of God. They expressed their faith that God had miraculously delivered His people before, and that He was still able to do the same for them. *"O LORD God of our fathers, art not thou God in heaven? and rulest not thou over all the kingdoms of the heathen? and in thine hand is there not power and might, so that none is able to withstand thee? Art not thou our God, who didst drive out the inhabitants of this land before thy people Israel, and gavest it to the seed of Abraham thy friend for ever?"* (v. 6-7) How much more might be accomplished in answer to our prayers if we truly had and expressed faith in God's power. They didn't say, "We know You can, we just don't know if You want to." They were in a desperate situation, so they prayed a desperate prayer. "Lord, help us!"

Notice, also, that they saw the importance of their prayer being in the right relationship to the house of God. *"If when evil cometh upon us, as the sword, judgment, or pestilence, or famine, we stand before this house, and in thy presence, (for thy name is in this house,) and cry unto thee in our affliction, then thou wilt hear and help."* (v. 9) In the Old Testament, the Temple was the house of God,

133

where God's Spirit dwelt among the people, and where blood sacrifice was made to demonstrate trust in the Blood of the Lamb, Who was slain from before the foundation of the world.

In the New Testament, God's Spirit dwells within the believer and the Blood Sacrifice has been offered up once for all. But Christ established His church upon Himself and promised that the gates of Hell would not prevail against it. I Timothy 3:15 identifies the church as the New Testament 'house of God'. *"...that thou mayest know how thou oughtest to behave thyself in the house of God, which is the church of the living God, the pillar and ground of the truth."* These believers realized the need of prayer being in harmony to a person's relationship with the house of God. I believe that this is still necessary today.

Although I don't think that only the prayers prayed inside the church can be answered, I have been taught that miraculous answers to prayer will not come to the believer who is continually and purposely in opposition to God's plan for believers to be active and cooperative in a local, Bible-believing church. If they get in a tight spot and need to pray, they will have to begin by confessing that they have been wrong, and they are willing to submit to God's plan for Christians to be a part of a local body of believers and serve with the pastor that God has given them. Christ didn't build His church for us to stay at home and do our own thing, nor to sit in the pew and critique and oppose everything that is done there. He established the church for us to be an active, cooperative member of the body. Our miraculous answers to prayer are directly affected by our relationship to the house of God.

Jehoshaphat and the people of Judah simply sought the Lord, recognizing their own weakness and the Lord's strength. "We don't know what to do," they said, "but our eyes are upon Thee." There we have the answer about "What Do You Do When You Don't Know What To Do?" The solution is simply to keep your eyes on the Lord. Wait on His answer, as these people did. God delights to show His mighty arm of power if only we will depend upon Him. The Lord spoke to Jehoshaphat through a man of God. *"Be not afraid nor dismayed by reason of this great multitude; for the battle is not yours, but God's...Ye shall not need to fight in this battle: set yourselves, stand ye still, and see the salvation of the LORD with you..." (v. 16-17)*

The next morning, the people of Judah expressed their faith in God's promise by going out to meet the great armies of Ammon and Moab. As they went, Jehoshaphat reassured them, *"Believe in the LORD your God, so shall ye be established; believe his prophets, so shall ye prosper." (v. 20)* Then Jehoshaphat appointed singers, and when they began to sing praises unto the Lord, God caused the enemy troops to destroy one another, so that none escaped alive. Not only did God's people have victory without ever having to fight, but the spoils of their triumph were so great that it took three days to gather the riches and precious jewels to carry them back home.

Keep your eyes on the Lord! Certainly this king of Judah learned his lesson about what to do when he didn't know what to do. May we also learn to look to the Lord. When circumstances look grim at best, and every option available seems to be the wrong one, may we learn to trust in the Omnipotence of our great God and say, as Jehoshaphat did: "Our eyes are upon Thee."

God Is Still On The Throne

When my heart is in distress
When the billows roll, and the burdens press,
I may not understand
just what my Lord has planned
But I know God is still on the throne.

At times my soul may be cast down
And the enemy is encamped around
When no hope I see, still I look to Thee,
For I know God, You're still on the throne.

I can still give God my praise
In the deepest nights and the darkest days,
For I know that He chooses best for me
And I know God is still on the throne.

God is still on the throne
And the Father still cares for His own.
Child, don't despair for the Lord is there
Yes, God is still on the throne.

by Cathy Corle

Chapter Sixteen

The Fault of Faultfinding

"And why beholdest thou the mote that is in thy brother's eye, but considerest not the beam that is in thine own eye? Or how wilt thou say to thy brother, Let me pull out the mote out of thine eye; and behold, a beam is in thine own eye? Thou hypocrite, first cast out the beam out of thine own eye; and then shalt thou see clearly to cast out the mote out of thy brother's eye." (Matthew 7:3-5)

Sometimes I think I am the only writer in America who 'preaches' to herself and just lets everyone else read the dialogue. For years I have been sharing something with ladies each month, and usually it is something I am experiencing or the Lord is teaching me at the time. When God speaks to me about something, I just assume that there may be someone else who is learning or needs to learn the same lessons that I need.

I don't know if any of these messages have helped or reproved anyone else much, but some of them have really torn me up! This is one of those 'ouchy' ones for me, but I feel like it may be needed. If you don't need it, I know that I do!

Some time ago I was in a preaching service, and also present was a man who had made some very critical and unfounded remarks about us and our ministry. Before the preaching began, I found myself hoping that the preacher would really 'load his wagon' and preach on his sin. As the preacher prayed after reading his text, I prayed, "Lord, you know how much I want to pray for you to give so and so just what he needs, but I know my attitude is not right. So Lord, just give me what I need."

That preacher, who knew nothing of the situation, preached the same message I would have liked to have written for him to preach to my critic, only he preached it a lot better than I could have imagined it. I found myself thinking, "But I asked for what I needed, not for what he needed." And all the time the Lord was rebuking me in my heart, saying that I needed it as much as he did. So guess who got their wagon loaded? Me!

In Matthew 7, Jesus was talking to religious people who had a high moral standard and lived by a very strict religious code. Like others with higher standards than the majority, they tended to 'look down their long Pharisaical noses' at everyone else who did not live up to their expectations. My husband has said, "Fundamentalists are funny creatures. Our attitude is: 'If you are guilty of the same sin I am, you're OK. But if you are guilty of a sin I haven't committed, you're BAD!'"

The Pharisees had the same problem. In essence He told them, "When you're looking for faults, use a mirror instead of a telescope." Don't be trying to correct the little faults of someone else until your own great big faults are all cared for. I'm sure Christ must have found just a little bit of humor in the idea of someone who had a beam in their eye, literally one of the supporting beams of the roof, trying to remove a small splinter from the eye of someone else. It is not so humorous when we stop to realize that most of us have been guilty of this very sin.

> **Before You Criticize:**
> **"When you are disposed to criticize a friend,**
> **Just remember, the beginning's not the end;**
> **When within this urge you find,**
> **These three questions bring to mind:**
> **Is it TRUE? Is it NEEDFUL? Is it KIND?"**

Many things have been said of criticism. "It is much easier to be critical than correct." "Criticism is easier than craftsmanship." "Nothing is easier than faultfinding: It takes no talent, no brains, no self-respect, and no character. All it takes is a big mouth." Oliver Wendell Holmes said: "The human race is divided into two classes -- those who go ahead and do something, and those who sit around and ask, 'Why wasn't it done the other way?'" These thoughts may help to expose and correct the Fault Of Faultfinding in our own lives.

1. I must realize that Jesus Christ had no faults, yet He was never critical and faultfinding with others. If the only Person Who ever was faultless did not take it upon Himself to spotlight the faults of others, how can I presume to do so? Faultfinding is as unChristlike as adultery and drunkenness, yet most of us feel very respectable to indulge in this sin. We may think that we have all our do's and don'ts down pat, but when we begin criticizing those who don't we have fallen into a sin more grievous than theirs. When Christians adopt an unChristian spirit, the soldiers of the cross are almost smug to find out that another soldier has fallen. Despite the fact that not one of us has any room to talk, the saying is true: "Some people are so polished. Everything they say reflects on somebody."

Jesus did not find fault. In fact the only people that he railed upon were the Pharisaical faultfinders! If I strive to be like Christ, then faultfinding must find its way out of my life, as well.

2. I must realize that I have have faults and imperfections just as glaring as the person I am tempted to criticize. Someone has given this wise advice: "Before criticizing another's faults, take time to count ten of your own...there will be plenty to choose from!" Another has added: "If you think you have no faults, that just makes one more." We need to get our eyes off the faults of others, and focus on correcting our own. There was only one faultless Person in history, and the Bible says He *"...is able...to present you faultless before the presence of his glory with exceeding joy." (Jude 24)*

How seldom we weigh our neighbor in the same balance with ourselves. This voice spoke from another century very pointedly. "Endeavor to be always patient of the faults and imperfections of others; for thou hast many faults and imperfections of thine own that require forbearance. If thou art not able to make thyself that which thou wishest, how can thou expect to mold another in conformity to thy will?"

How often have we heard someone's accusation of sin in another Christian, only to learn that the critic is guilty of the same trespass which he has condemned? Henrietta Mears spoke gravely of the predisposition to criticize in others what we ignore in ourselves. "So many times the faults we see in others are our own. If we tell lies, we are watching and anxious to see another person tell an untruth. If we are selfish, we delight to see selfishness in others." A judge repeated this warning: "Criticizing others is a

140

dangerous thing, not so much because you may make mistakes about them, but because you may be revealing the truth about yourself."

Have you noticed?...When someone else acts a certain way, it's rudeness; but when you act that way, it's nerves? When others are set in their ways, it's obstinance; but when you are, it's firmness? When your neighbor doesn't like your friend, it's prejudice; but when you don't like him, it's good judgment of character? When someone else takes their time, it's laziness; but when you do, it's carefulness? When he notices a flaw, he's cranky; but when you do, you're observant? When someone else dresses well, it's extravagance; but when you do, it's tastefulness? When he speaks his mind, he's spiteful; but when you do, you're honest? My, how the faults of others look virtuous when we see them in ourselves!

Many times I have heard criticism of myself or others, when I knew of circumstances the critic did not know that changed the outlook considerably. Suppose you were to hear criticism of a lady who is not faithful to all the services of the church, and then learn that she has an unsaved husband that forbids her and makes her life unbearable when she does come? We need to remember this time-tested prayer: "Lord, teach me never to judge another until I have walked two weeks in his shoes." If you don't know all, then don't say any! We all have faults equally as bad as those we can find to critique in others.

3. I must realize that the instances when others criticize me will be the most tempting times for me to criticize them in return. In researching for this article, I realized that great Christians are always people who are sorely criticized, and the greatest Christians are those who resist the temptation to criticize their critics. It is so tempting for us to 'Do unto others what they've already

141

done to us.'

Yet Jesus did not retaliate, and neither should we. *"For even hereunto were ye called: because Christ also suffered for us, leaving us an example, that ye should follow his steps:..Who, when he was reviled, reviled not again..."* (1 Peter 2:21,23) It has been said that the only sure way to avoid criticism is to say nothing, do nothing, and be nothing. Anyone who accomplishes something in the work of God will be met by criticism. It is not nearly as important what our critics say about us, as what we say in return.

The following is quoted from a 19th century book: "Silence is often the best answer to criticism. Sometimes a man's steady, faithful work is his defense. Violinist Ole' Bull was once offered space in the New York Herald to answer his detractors, but declined saying, 'I think it is best that they write against me and I play against them.' The finest argument against criticism is a faithful doing of the very best one can do. It disarms criticism. It wins sympathy and admiration. It wastes no time and suffers no loss. Practical doing is ever better than faultfinding or trying to satisfy the censorious, and the whole world knows it."

One of the many antagonists of the early days of the Salvation Army was the brilliant Thomas H. Huxley, biologist and agnostic. Through the letter columns of the London Times, Huxley launched an all-out attack on General William Booth and his organization. He saw Booth as a manipulator of the minds of his followers and termed it a 'prostitution of the mind.' He reasoned that Booth's sway over the soldiers was an evil worse than harlotry or intemperance.

Others followed Huxley in his frequent blasts at Booth and the Salvation Army. Booth's enemies were most

142

generous with invectives, a practice that angered Bramwell Booth, the general's son.

The elder Booth reasoned with Bramwell that he couldn't waste time fighting his critics. He would not be diverted from what he felt God wanted him to do. "Bramwell," he said, "fifty years hence it will matter very little indeed how these people treated us. It will matter a great deal how we dealt with the work of God." How convincingly time has proved his statement to be true!

Abraham Lincoln was questioned about his silence in response to the constant criticism he received. His answer? "If I tried to read, much less answer all the criticisms made of me, and all the attacks leveled against me, this office would have to be closed for all other business. I do the best I know how, the very best I can. And I mean to keep on doing this, down to the very end. If the end brings me out all wrong, ten angels swearing I had been right would make no difference. If the end brings me out all right, then what is said against me now will not amount to anything." How many of us remember what was said against him? How many of us remember what he did? History often speaks for itself.

As Robert E. Lee conversed with Jefferson Davis one day, he spoke of a certain man with the highest regard and praise for his ability. An officer who overheard the conversation was shocked and asked, "General, do you not know that the man of whom you speak so highly is one of your bitterest enemies and misses no opportunity to malign you?" "Yes," replied General Lee, "but the President asked for my opinion of him. He did not ask for his opinion of me."

When Plato was told that many of his enemies slandered him, he replied, "It is no matter. I shall live so that none will believe them." One man advised, "What should you do

143

about criticism? If it is untrue, disregard it. If it is unfair, don't be irritated by it. If it is ignorant, smile at it. If it is justified, learn from it. But never, oh never, return it." It is true. Nobody raises his own reputation by trying to lower another's.

When you're criticizing others
And are finding here and there
A fault or two to speak of, or a weakness you can tear;
When you're blaming someone's meanness
Or accusing one of pelf --
It's time that you went out to take a walk around yourself.

There's lots of human failures in the average of us all,
And lots of grave shortcomings
In the short ones and the tall;
But when we think of evils
Men should lay upon the shelves,
It's time we all went out to take a walk around ourselves.

We need so often in this life this balancing of the scales,
This seeing how much in us wins
And how much in us fails;
Before you judge another -- just to lay him on the shelf --
It would be a splendid plan
To take a walk around yourself.
(Helen Welshimer)

Worse than the sin that we criticize is the sin of criticism. We need to get our eyes open to the fact that derogatory speaking of others, called by any name, is still wrong. When we find fault with others, we demonstrate that we also have a fault that needs correcting, The Fault Of Faultfinding.

144

Chapter Seventeen

Quitting Insurance

One day I was musing over the thought that, as well as finances would allow, most people are pretty well prepared for many of the unpleasant things that might happen in the future. There is fire insurance in case we have a fire, car insurance in case we have an accident, health insurance in case someone has a sickness or injury that puts them into the hospital, even life insurance to help out in case of the death of the bread winner.

Now, we're not sitting around waiting for any of those things to happen right now. We don't know that we'll ever face any of those things in our lifetime. But insurance is just a provision made ahead of time so that you're better prepared when you face one of those tragedies. Without it, any one of those circumstances might leave you financially devastated.

I thought, "I wish I could sell marriage insurance, so folks could be guaranteed that their marriage would never break up, or child-training insurance, to guard against our children turning away from all we've taught them and wrecking their lives in sin once they're grown. What about friendship insurance, to prevent your closest companions from someday turning against you and breaking your heart. Or maybe...?"

Well, you see the direction in which my thoughts were wandering, anyway. It occurred to me that one of the greatest concerns in my life is that I'll quit. Quit the ministry. Quit living for God. Quit on my marriage and my children. All around me, I've seen people throwing in the towel and leaving pain and devastation in their wake, and I don't want to join them now or 50 years from now. I'm not talking about bad people, or people who had bad motives, or unspiritual, uncharactered Christians. Over the years many folks who I've admired and looked to for example and teaching have now turned aside, and I'm sure that some of them were at one time stronger and more dedicated Christians than me. I know myself too well to think that I'm above falling into the same traps that have wrecked these dear folks. Not for one minute do I intend to be critical or judgmental of someone who has already quit, yet I would like to learn from their mistakes and guard against them in my own life. But how do you protect yourself against quitting?

Now, when do you buy an insurance policy? Do you wait until tragedy strikes? Or until you are sure that trouble is on the way? No, insurance is a preparation that you make in fair weather because you know that someday a storm may come. If I'm going to fortify my 'stick-to-it-ivity' and be prepared to weather the storms without sinking to the bottom, then I'm going to have to make some preparations and provisions against quitting during a time when quitting is the furthest thing from my mind. So here's a few thoughts that make up my 'rough-draft' in hope that you'll be able to perfect the idea, and it will be a strength and encouragement to you somewhere down the road when you most need it.

1. Realize and admit that you WILL be tempted to quit.

"And the Lord said, Simon, Simon, behold, Satan hath desired to have you, that he may sift you as wheat: But I have prayed for thee, that thy faith fail not: and when thou art converted, strengthen thy brethren." *(Luke 22:31-32)* A person must be either very conceited or VERY naive if they think they'll never face the heart-break and discouragement that have brought others to their lowest ebb and prompted them to quit on God. I know that I'm not any more spiritual, and I'm certain that I'm not as strong as Moses, or Elijah, or Jeremiah, or Jonah, or Peter. Yet all of these good servants of God came to a point where they wanted to quit. One of the best defenses against the temptation to quit is to anticipate it, so that it will not be nearly as surprising or as painful.

2. Realize why you're tempted to quit.

In one way, the devil's onslaught can be an encouragement. The devil is not fighting the folks who are doing nothing. He wants to ruin those who are doing the most damage to his plans. I'm convinced that Satan works harder to destroy the marriages of fundamental, soulwinning preachers and their wives than just about anyone else in the world. He spends all of his time and energy trying to stir up strife and ill-will in a separated, soulwinning church while many liberal churches seem to be peaceful. If the devil attacks you with discouragement, then you must be doing something right. Be sure and give him the credit he deserves, instead of thinking it's all your husband, your friend, your preacher, or your mother.

As ladies, we may as well admit that we've got the

147

added problem of roller-coaster emotions to cope with. We need to admit to ourselves that sometimes the problem is not with us or with anyone else, but its just the fact that we're faced with many more ups-and-downs in our feelings and moods than men have to deal with. When it's appropriate, don't hesitate to relegate the blame to that fact instead of blaming everything and everybody else around you.

3. Be prepared with some special verses and Bible illustrations that will bolster your resolve to keep on keeping on.

"I can do all things through Christ which strengtheneth me." (Philippians 4:13) "And we know that all things work together for good to them that love God, to them who are the called according to his purpose." (Romans 8:28) "And let us not be weary in well doing: for in due season we shall reap, if we faint not." (Galatians 6:9) "Therefore seeing we have this ministry, as we have received mercy, we faint not... But we have this treasure in earthen vessels, that the excellency of the power may be of God, and not of us. We are troubled on every side, yet not distressed; we are perplexed, but not in despair; Persecuted, but not forsaken; cast down, but not destroyed;" (II Corinthians 4:1, 7-10) You'll find a gold mine of encouragement when you start digging it out of the Bible.

I also know of some books and sermon tapes that have been especially encouraging to me in the past, and I often refer to those in memory, and sometimes even go hunting them up to let them encourage me all over again. A sermon that was preached by Dr. Bob Kelley about the importance of what you say to yourself is one that God used at a crucial time in my life, and the Lord has used the points of that message time after time to get me thinking on the right track again. Dr. Hyles recently preached a message on a wounded spirit, and I needed the instruction that it gave me. The Holy Spirit was saying, "See, there... what did I tell you!" There are songs that mean something special to me. I have gotten through some trying days to the tune of 'Day By Day' or 'My Faith Has Found A Resting Place.' There are messages I've written for the paper in years gone by about the encouraging things that God has taught me from His Word, and I find myself re-reading those precious lessons again. Those verses and books and sermons and songs are all things I count on for 'insurance.'

4. Make God some promises about finishing what he has for you to do.

No matter what you're doing, if you have a tentative attitude about it, you're destined to quit sooner or later, and it will probably be sooner. Promise God, "Lord, I will not quit!" Whatever He has given you to do, make some promises about it. The Lord has given us a ministry that requires being on the road at times and being separated at other times. Some days things go pretty smooth... and then there are other days! God has given us the privilege to have a *Revival Fires!* and the opportunity to see it be a blessing and encouragement to countless people. There are many, many blessings, yet I'd be dishonest if I said I've never been tempted to quit. My service to God requires me to deal with a different set of responsibilities and people than yours does, and vice-versa. If you're in any type of ministry, you'll get disgruntled and upset with people, often the very people that you're supposed to be teaching and helping. But promise God that no matter what happens, you won't quit, and when you're tempted to quit, that promise will be a reminder and a motivator to stick it out.

Over the years I've made and re-made many promises to the Lord, and every time the devil has whispered, "Quit," the Lord has reminded me about them. One that I particularly remember was made outside a little motel in Batesville, Arkansas with my 3 month old baby in her little seat beside me. God brings that instance to my mind very often. I've found it especially important to make promises to God concerning my relationships and ministry to others, especially my husband and children. That way, if I feel I've been wronged, I'm reminded that I've promised to do right as a wife or mother, and made that promise to God. Sometimes I can say, "Lord, I'm doing this for you," even if it takes a while for me to be able to be what I ought to be for the sake of that person alone.

5. Guard your weaknesses and times of temptation.

Everyone has heard it said that one of the most likely times to face discouragement is right after a great victory in your life, and that is so true. Because we've been warned about that over and over, we're usually on our guard at those vulnerable times, and maybe even adjust our schedule to better cope with it. But that's not the only situation that consistently brings discouragement or fatigue or bitterness or any of the countless other things that lead to quitting.

You can probably think of certain holidays or events that usually leave you drained and despondent. You can probably spout off the names of several people who are not the best influence on your spiritual state. Whether it's prompted by sickness, or the Christmas season, or spring fever, or the most exciting day of your life, or a visit from your least favorite in-law, you can prepare yourself to fight off the temptation to quit.

6. Adjust your philosophy to admit that it's better to fail

than to quit.

I have to admit that this was not one of the easier points for me. I was the one in high school who if I didn't get an A, didn't care if I got an F. I've learned over the years that the fear of failure can keep you from ever starting, and if you are going to do something for God with your life, you'll have to take some chances with the attitude that 'failure is the only means by which you can start over more intelligently.' I really do think that sometimes people are faced with a situation where they think others will view them or their ministry as a failure, so instead they quit. Yet if I get my eyes on God's perspective of my life, it's much more honorable to 'fail' while trying to do something right, than to quit in my endeavors to serve the Lord. I think God honors that kind of attitude.

7. Surround yourself with encouragement.

Being a poet of sorts, I find poetry especially encouraging and uplifting when I'm in need of it. I have several poems scribbled into my Bible margins and hanging on the wall around my work area. I've written some poems like "Don't Worry Robin" that are encouraging, not because they're so good, but because they're so real to me and the circumstances that prompted me to write them are still vivid in my memory. There are many little notes from my girls, and special little gifts and cards from my husband tacked up all over where I can see them. I count these little scraps of paper and cards and notes and reminders as some of the most crucial components of my plan of protection. From where I sit right now I can see many of these, as well as a little vase that says, "You're very special to me," and a coloring book picture of a secretary slumped over a typewriter complete with "Dear Mom --- I love you" written in crayon across the top. Maybe that's not the kind

151

of thing that is a breath of fresh air to you when you're smothering in discouragement, but whatever is, keep it available.

8. Laugh so you won't cry, or cry if you must.

A friend of mine, Marilyn Cunningham, recently gave me a card that pictures a gorilla with bubble gum stringing from mouth to hands to feet and simply says, "Stick to it!" Thank you, I will! I enjoy funny little things like that, and often a chance to laugh at your plight is all you need to get that mountainous burden back down to mole-hill size where it belongs. My mother sent me two little posters that I especially like. One with a bursting file cabinet, overflowing trash can, phone receiver hanging off and lots of stray paper says, "I'm over-worked and under-slept." The other says, "I try to take one day at a time... but lately I've been attacked by several days at once!" One of my favorites is a picture of two fear-stricken fish swimming in a blender with their eye on the plug in the electric socket, and says, "I can't stand the tension in here!" Sometimes a break with someone who's alot of fun, if rather crazy, can be just the antidote needed to fight off a bad case of end-of-my-rope fever. Anything to help me lighten up and laugh a little is much appreciated at a time like that.

But there are times when you just have to cry, and when that time comes, don't mistake it for the end of the world. Just have a good cry, pray about it, and go on. That may be the best thing you can do.

9. Remember why you started in the first place.

Starting is the exact opposite of quitting, right? When you started, what was your purpose, your motivation, your aim? If you're despairing over your marriage, stop and think over those sweet and exciting times that prompted you to promise, 'for better or for worse.' What were some of the things that thrilled your heart then? Somewhere under all the rush and routine, the same two people still exist who were so much in love back then, and so determined make each other happy.

I have many friends who, like me, are home schooling. That is one of the most rewarding as well as one of the most taxing endeavors you'll ever undertake. On a day that's less-than-ideal, it's helpful to think back to those baby days when I thanked the Lord continually for allowing me to have a part in bringing up His servants, and resolved to pay the price to protect them from the world, and bring them up in the nurture and admonition of the Lord.

When your spirits are lagging over your ministry for the Lord, and people have used you and mistreated you, and things are not moving along as quickly or smoothly as they should, it's time to refocus your attention back to where it used to be. Remember when you thought it would be the most thrilling thing in the world if God could use YOU? Back when any little thing you could do for the Lord was a sheer delight? Why are you entertaining the idea of quitting? Did God hurt you, or was it just people? If God has never done you any wrong, why would you quit on Him? Because our service to God often centers around serving people for God, we can get needlessly out of sorts if we're not careful. If you quit, it won't be nearly so hurtful to the people who've hurt you as it will be to the Savior who bought you with His blood.

10. List God's promises, claim them, and fight to stay positive.

Every promise in the Book IS mine. *"What shall we then say to these things? If God be for us, who can be against us? He that spared not his own Son, but delivered*

153

him up for us all, how shall he not with him also freely give us all things?" (Romans 8:31-32) "Now unto him that is able to do exceeding abundantly above all that we ask or think, according to the power that worketh in us, Unto him be glory in the church by Christ Jesus throughout all ages, world without end. Amen." (Ephesians 3:20-21) "But thanks be to God, which giveth us the victory through our Lord Jesus Christ. Therefore my beloved brethren, be ye stedfast, unmoveable, always abounding in the work of the Lord, forasmuch as ye know that your labour is not in vain in the Lord." (I Corinthians 15:57-58)

11. Count your blessings, then demand a recount.

I never get tired of talking over and thinking over the many, many answers to prayer we've seen in our ministry. During the first year of our marriage I kept a list in my Bible of blessings and answers to prayer, and I still marvel every time I read over it. They say that, "Contentment is the art of enjoying what you have." If I get my eyes off of what I don't have and on what I do have, things will brighten up. If I stop spending all my time and energy stewing over the things that have gone awry, and stop to think about all the wonderful things that haven't, I won't be nearly so discouraged. The Bible often rehearses the past miracles and victories of God's people, which ought to remind us that we need the same kind of encouragement.

"Count your blessings, name them one by one, Count your many blessings, see what God hath done."

12. Have an 'in case of emergency' plan.

I have a friend named Sharon who lives in West Virginia. I've often told her, "You're one of the few friends who, if I were in prison for murder, I know you'd be standing at my cell swearing I didn't do it." I don't get to see her very often, but she's a true, dear friend and I love her. I've said to myself many times, "If I ever HAVE to talk to someone, I know I could call Sharon." Do you know how many times I've called her to pour out my woes? Zero! Just knowing that I could has always been enough.

Mrs. Joe Boyd told me of a time when her mother was very ill and she was as low as she'd been in many years. Brother Boyd had told her, "If you ever really need me, you just let me know, and I promise I'll come home." Out of more than 40 years, that was the one time that she collected on that promise, and knowing that he would come if she asked was often comfort in itself.

I guess everybody could have a plan to use 'in case of emergency.' We may never come to that point, but knowing that there would be a relief in sight if we did is a great comfort. When Elijah faced the deepest valley of his life, God thought it important enough to send an angel to care for his needs. There is always an answer, whether it's a simple, visible solution like a phone call, or a miracle that only God can perform. *"There hath no temptation taken you but such as is common to man: but God is faithful, who will not suffer you to be tempted above that ye are able; but will with the temptation also make a way to escape, that ye may be able to bear it." (I Corinthians 10:13)* You never have to quit.

Not long ago I spent some time over pizza with three young preachers' wives whose husbands recently graduated from Bible college. Before the conversation was over, one of them asked, "What is one main word of advice you would give to a young preacher's wife?" I'm sure they were expecting something much more dramatic than my answer. I said, "That's easy. Just do what God wants you to do, do it 'as unto the Lord,' and don't ever quit. The times will come when that's all the advice you can handle, and if you do quit, no other advice will be of any value."

If you're facing discouragement, and the devil's been suggesting that you just quit, I trust that I've thrown you the life-preserver you need. Just don't quit!

I hope, rather, that you're reading this without any inkling of discontentment or discouragement to mar your joy in serving God. I assure you that you can expect many more blessings than trials. It's just that our human nature tends to magnify the trials when they come, and let them hide all the blessings from view. Insurance is that provision you make for stormy weather when the sky is clear and the water is calm. So let these ideas be the first installment in your policy of 'Quitting Insurance,' and tuck them away where they can be found when they're needed. And Just Don't Quit!

DON'T QUIT!

When things go wrong, as they sometimes will,
And the road you're trudging seems all uphill,
When the funds are low, and the debts are high,
And you want to smile, but you have to sigh;
When care is pressing you down a bit,
Rest if you must, but DON'T YOU QUIT!

Success is failure turned inside out
The silver tint to the clouds of doubt
You never can tell how close you are --
It may be near when it seems afar.
So stick to the fight when you're hardest hit.
It's when things go wrong that
YOU MUST NOT QUIT!

Chapter Eighteen

The Bottom Line

"Whether therefore ye eat, or drink, or whatsoever ye do, do all to the glory of God." (I Corinthians 10:31)
"And whatsoever ye do in word or deed, do all in the name of the Lord Jesus, giving thanks to God and the Father by Him." (Colossians 3:17)

Maybe a more appropriate title for these thoughts would be "How to insure your future for God" or "How to keep doing what you've been doing." Anybody who has read much of what I've written has probably noticed a train of thought that often threads its way into my topics of conversation. So many people have quit -- so many good people -- so many have given up the fight against the devil, given in to sin and temptation, given over to less important ideals and philosophies. How can I be sure that I'm not going to do the same thing somewhere along the line?

Brother Cham McMillen, a pastor in Florida, gave me a lot of food for thought when he said something like this.

"Over the years, the things that have been my biggest goals and desires and longings have either been fulfilled or replaced or forgotten. And as I grow older, I find my greatest goal and desire is that I'll finish like I started. I want to die still being faithful to the Lord. That has become the goal that I'm striving for."

I know that I have plenty of room for growth, to aim higher and do more, and I certainly want to do that. But I fear that sometimes we lose our perspective on the importance of faithfulness. Constant focus on superlatives bring the temptation that "If I can't break last year's record, then maybe I ought to just quit." Faithfulness is important in and of itself, and if I can't win more souls this year than I did last year, I certainly ought to do my best and win as many as I can. History has proven again and again that faithfulness and consistency and persistence always win out over the drive to be the biggest, fastest, and greatest. We need to put a premium on faithfulness, and add our motivation to excel on top of it, not in place of it.

I want to finish like I've started, or better. Yet I have the constant reminders of my own weakness and inabilities. I see the dangers and the possibilities present with me all the time. David said, *"For I acknowledge my transgressions: and my sin is ever before me."* (Psalm 51:3) Paul said, *"For I know that in me (that is, in my flesh,) dwelleth no good thing: for to will is present with me; but how to perform that which is good I find not."* (Romans 7:18) Since these two men, some of the greatest men of God in all of history, struggled with their own weakness and sinfulness, where does that leave me? Sometimes I feel like I belong in the 'endangered species' category, for sure!

This is just one idea of many that has been turned over and over in my mind, and since I think it has strengthened and encouraged me, maybe it will have some value for

158

somebody else, as well.

Motivation is a key word in your service to the Lord, and in living right and doing right in the face of constant pressure to do otherwise. Anyone who serves the Lord and lives a godly life and raises a family and builds a marriage over the course of many years will have something to share with you about what motivates them to do what they're doing. Nobody will do what God wants them to do 'just because' or 'because so-and-so says to do this.' There has to be something stronger, deeper, and more eternal behind our service to God or it won't last.

Motives are important. They're important to God, because He sees the heart behind the actions, the desires behind the doing. Three people may be doing the same thing, for example, teaching a class, and all of their efforts might be similarly used and appreciated in the church. But suppose, for instance, that one of them was motivated by a desire to be seen and appreciated by people, or even a longing to fit in and do what others are doing in the church. Another might be trying to help the preacher, and doing what he asked them to do. Another person might be acting out of a heart of love for the Lord, and a desire to serve Him and bring glory to Him in this world. I think the truth might be evident long before, but if not, I'm sure there is a difference in their rewards when they stand before the Lord at the Judgment Seat of Christ, even though their actions were the same.

Motives are important to the Lord, and He sees deep into our hearts. We may learn when we get to Heaven that it was not even possible for our sinful, human selves to be entirely free from the wrong desires and motives. But I'm sure that it's possible for us to try, and to be as sincere and Christ-honoring as we can possibly be, and to devote our hearts to God as well as our hands to His work.

159

But I've learned that my motives are not only important to God. They're very important to me, as well. My motives for what I'm doing, or one of my motives, might be the one thin string that keeps me hanging on just long enough in a desperate moment. Even on a daily basis, my motives not only determine what I do, but they're a pretty good indicator of how long I'll keep doing it and what price I'll be willing to pay, if and when it becomes necessary.

Picture this in your mind. Your motives in life are in 'layers.' Anything that is a big part of your life, that is an important part of your service and responsibility to God, will have more than just one motivation behind it. Whether it be soulwinning, Bible reading, church attendance, child-training, marriage, or any other thing you want to fill in the blank, if you have a little heart to heart talk with yourself, you'll find out you have several reasons for why you're doing what you're doing.

One illustration of my point might be in raising my children. That entails physical care, household responsibilities, spending time with my children, taking them to church and soulwinning, discipline and training, and for me it includes schoolwork, as well. Why do I keep on doing all those things? Well, because I love my children, because I want what's best for them, because I want to be close to them, because I want them to be happy, because I want them to grow up to be the kind of adult Christians that I can be proud of, because I want them to serve and honor and glorify the Lord with their lives, because I want them to have happy marriages and homes and children someday... I could probably go on for quite a while. Maybe I ought to list some more selfish reasons, so that you can understand my illustration better, like being proud of them, desiring their love and affection, and so on.

Now, the bottom line of my motivation in any area has

to be to bring glory to the Lord. That is the basis of the Christian life. That's why we're here. *"Whether therefore ye eat, or drink, or whatsoever ye do, do all to the glory of God."* *(I Corinthians 10:31)* *"What? know ye not that your body is the temple of the Holy Ghost, which is in you, which ye have of God, and ye are not your own? For ye are bought with a price: therefore glorify God in your body, and in your spirit, which are God's."* *(I Corinthians 6:19-20)* *"And whatsoever ye do in word or deed, do all in the name of the Lord Jesus, giving thanks to God and the Father by Him."* *(Colossians 3:17)* *"And whatsoever ye do, do it heartily, as to the Lord, and not unto men. Knowing that of the Lord ye shall receive the reward of the inheritance: for ye serve the Lord Christ. And he that doeth wrong shall receive for the wrong which he hath done: and there is no respect of persons."* *(Colossians 3:23)*

If I don't have the glory of God as the bottom line in any area, then it's missing the strong foundation that is necessary. Whatever area of life you're struggling with right now, wherever the devil is fighting you the hardest, stop and think about your motivation to honor and glorify God in that situation. What is it that God desires and expects from you? What is the right, God-honoring thing to do? For many of us, it's just to keep on doing what you've been doing. JUST DON'T QUIT!

But those other layers have some value and strength, too. Nobody is 100% spiritual and right with God 24 hours a day all seven days of the week. Backsliding, or at least getting cold-hearted, is an ever-present threat. When you're no longer doing right for the best and highest reason, you may fall back on a less spiritual reason, or a more selfish reason. But if that keeps you doing what you're doing for one more week, one more day, or one more hour, it gives you the opportunity to examine your heart, get alone with God, pray and read God's Word, and get yourself back on track, back into the situation where you're doing what God wants you to do for the best and highest reason -- for His glory.

Probably everyone who is reading this has experienced it to some extent, but you may not have thought about the truth behind it. The more layers of motivation I have in doing what's right, the greater my protection. When one is destroyed, there's another to fall back on. The foundational purpose or the 'bottom line' for all of what we do has got to be for the glory of God. In your marriage, in motherhood, in separation, in doing right in response to wrong that's done against you, you name it. When all your other motivations cease to keep you going, keep on doing what's right because it's right, and because it will honor God, and because God will reward doing right.

In everything that we do for God, we ought to be doing it for His glory, in obedience to His instructions, empowered by His Spirit, begging for His wisdom and power and intervention and miracles and success. Bringing glory to God and living for Him and serving Him and pleasing Him ought to be on our minds and hearts everyday in everything that we do. BUT... you know 'meanwhile, back at the ranch,' are other things that we have to deal with, too. So there are other motives, or layers to our motivation, that are just as real.

Another truth that I've discovered is that goals or motives have directing power in our lives. Some goals are inherently good and godly, while others will always lead you in the wrong direction. For instance, I talked with a lady who for years served the Lord alone, married to an unsaved husband. It seemed that little she said or did had much influence on him to want the Lord in his heart and life. But over the course of time, she found that he had a desire and motivation for his children to attend the Christian school at their church. He had grown up in a godless home environment, and he felt very strongly that he wanted better for his own children. Now that is a good, godly goal, even in the heart of an unsaved man, and in time it led to his conversion. He is now a faithful deacon and bus driver in that church.

But you know, I've seen very good people get side-tracked by the motivation to have a lot of money, and that motive always leads people in the wrong direction. It's not the money that's dangerous, but the love of it that God said is 'the root of all evil.' Every preacher you know could name you at least a dozen families who were once some of the best workers in his church, but the desire for money and things got a hold of their hearts, and in time it pulled them away. Your motivation, the goals and desires that you entertain in your mind, will provide some of the direction that determines which way your life will go in the future.

Now let me reason with you from the opposite end of the same conversation. The first idea that caused me to spend a little time munching on this thought was the cold, hard fact that many good people are doing the right things for the wrong reasons, and don't even realize it. Maybe it's not necessarily a wrong reason, but it's not the best reason, or even one of the top ten! Those good people doing good things are endangering their service to God and the longevity of their faithfulness unless they take some time to add the more important 'layers' to their motivation to keep doing what they're already doing.

Separation is a prime example of what I'm talking about. There are hundreds of people in good Bible preaching churches who are living by the right standards 'because the preacher says so.' That's not a bad motivation, but it certainly won't last by itself. Until they examine the Bible verses that the preacher has been teaching them and say, "It's not just what the preacher says, it's what God says, too," their right-doing is in danger because it doesn't have a strong enough foundation. The answer is not to quit doing the right thing. The answer is to transfer our motivation for why we're doing the right thing, or to add to the 'good' reason that's not good enough all by itself.

Please realize that I'm not condemning anybody, but I'm warning everybody, especially me. You know, I don't think I've ever met one person who got saved for the purpose of bringing glory to God. Most everybody I know got saved just because they realized they were on their way to hell, and didn't want to go there. I even know a few people who got saved because they wanted forgiveness and relief from the guilt of their sin. I don't think God minded that at all. But after we get saved, it seems like every time we hear a message, and every time we read the Bible, we learn some wonderful new truth about what happened to us the day we got saved. God did save us to bring glory to Him, but most of us didn't learn that until quite some time later. Growing in knowledge and growing in strength are a natural part of the Christian life, and I think growing or 'adding layers' to our motivation and protection for our service to God is part of that growth.

You know, most of us married the right person but for the wrong reasons -- or at least not the best reasons. A lot of people get married because they have an innate longing to share oneness of life and future with a 'special someone,' because they want to be loved and cared for, because they experience physical attraction and desires. Maybe some are even motivated by a longing for security, or a fear of loneliness, or any other number of things. It's important for us to realize that God was the one who placed those needs

164

and desires and longings in our hearts, and He designed marriage to be the fulfillment of them.

But we need to learn that 'that's not all there is.' Marriage was the very first institution God ordained, before the parent-child relationship, even before the church. The only relationship that preceded it was the relationship between God and man. I think within the context of marriage is one of the most important areas of 'ministry' and opportunity to serve and please God that exists in any relationship or situation in life. Some of us have never once thought of our marriage as an opportunity and responsibility to please and glorify and honor and serve God. Some of us have even considered that truth in the abstract or the ideal, but I'm afraid very, very few of us have ever looked at our own marriage, our own relationship to the man we're married to, and the nitty-gritty situations we're facing in marriage today, and said, "I'm doing what I'm doing for the glory of God."

Because many of the natural instincts and needs that contribute to romance and 'falling in love' are based on 'my needs, my desires, my dreams, and my longings,' it's a temptation to live your entire married life based on selfish motivation. But what happens when your needs are no longer being met, when you no longer feel the 'tingle' you once felt, when your dreams are disillusioned, and maybe even crushed? If your ONLY motivation for doing the right thing in your marriage is selfish, then you've lost all your reasons for doing right. There's not much to hold you, and now you're in danger.

But if you add the common-sense and honorable motivations that people have acknowledged for years, you'll have some added protection for your marriage. When you said, "Till death do us part," you gave your word, your promise. You made a holy vow to God. If you're honest, you'll do everything in your power to fulfill your promise, and hang on to the very last shred of hope. "But I'm not happy, and I deserve to be happy." You didn't promise "till unhappiness sets in." You ought to feel the obligation of keeping your vows to God and to your husband.

"For the children" is not all bad to consider. It may not be good enough by itself, but I think it would benefit every single unhappy mother in the world a great deal if she would stop and realize the devastation that divorce will bring to her children's entire lives -- not just now, but until the day they die, and in every relationship they ever have. I've been good and angry more than once when I've seen the pain that a self-centered mother has inflicted on her child's heart just because she's discontented. Love for your children will keep you going, when your own reasons have crumbled.

"What will people think?" is pretty poor and selfish on it's own, but it is nevertheless a real part of everyone's life and future. We ought to be genuinely concerned about our testimony, about the influence that we'll have on others if we do wrong or fail to do right. We ought to consider the hurt and the discouragement that will come to the hearts of others if we surrender to the devil.

But underneath it all, we need to come to the realization and commitment that we're going to keep doing right because it's right, and because we want to honor and please God. "For the glory of God" is the foundational motive that ought to support all the other layers, in every area, including staying married, and doing right in our marriage, and building a godly, sweet, Christ-centered relationship within our marriage.

We all have those desires and needs for love and romance and oneness and that longing to be cherished and treasured and protected by the man we love. Those are not wrong desires, they're just not enough. If that's all the motivation you have for what you're doing, even though you're doing all the right things, the day may come when those motivations are non-existent in your marriage, or at least buried under the burdens of everyday life. When those things that motivate us have disappeared from view, we'll bail out unless we've added some important layers of protection to why we're doing what we're doing.

Why are you doing what you're doing? I challenge you to take some time to consider that thought, and consider the most important ministries and people that God has placed in your life. The more layers of motivation that you have, the more protection you have against the onslaught of the devil. And always, "for the glory of God" is the bottom line.

"But he that is greatest among you shall be your servant. And whosoever shall exalt himself shall be abased; and he that shall humble himself shall be exalted." (Matthew 23:12)

IF YOU WERE TO DIE TODAY, ARE YOU 100% SURE THAT YOU WOULD GO TO HEAVEN? If you could know that, you would want to, wouldn't you? Please take a few moments and let me share with you how the Bible says that you can know...

"Wherefore, as by one man sin entered into the world, an death by sin: and so death passed upon all men, for that all have sinned:" *(Romans 5:12)* The one thing that stands between us and going to Heaven when we die is our sin --- and God said that ALL have sinned. He didn't leave anyone out. If I'm going to be honest with myself, I must admit that I am included. I am a sinner first of all because I inherited a sinful nature from Adam that has been passed down to me. I am a sinner because I have disobeyed the clear commands of God. Just as it only takes one instance of stealing to make me a thief, it takes only one sin to make me a sinner. There are no 'good sinners' or 'bad sinners' in the eyes of God --- we all stand guilty before Him, and unworthy of Heaven.

The Bible says that there is a penalty for sin --- DEATH. *"...and so death passed upon all men, for that all have sinned."* *(Romans 5:12)* *"for the wages of sin is death..."* *(Romans 6:23)* You cannot pay for sin by going to church or being baptized or doing good deeds or keeping commandments. The only payment that will clear your account is death. This is not just a physical death. They Bible is clear that after the body dies, there is a second death or a spiritual death.

"But the fearful, and unbelieving, and the abominable, and murderers, and whoremongers, and

169

sorcerers, and idolaters, and all liars, shall have their part in the lake which burneth with fire and brimstone which is the second death." (Revelation 21:8) The Bible is clear that if we must pay the price for our sin, we must suffer a second death forever in the lake of fire called hell. No other payment that we can make would pay the price, because the wages of sin is death.

God loves us so much that He did not want us to go to hell, even though we deserve to do so. Yet he would not be just and righteous if He allowed us to go to Heaven with our sin, just as a judge would be unjust to let a murderer go free just because it was someone he knew and loved. Sin must be paid for. There is only one way for our sin to be paid for without you and I spending all eternity in the torment of Hell: to let Someone else pay the price for us.

"For God so loved the world, that he gave his only begotten Son, that whosoever believeth in him should not perish, but have everlasting life." (John 3:16) God allowed His Son, Jesus Christ, to suffer and die in our place to pay the price of death that we owe. We do not need to do anything to earn it, we must simply receive the salvation that Jesus paid for with His blood. *"But as many as received him, to them gave he power to become the sons of God, even to them that believe on his name:" (John 1:12)* If we will receive Jesus and His death on the cross as payment for our sins, He has promised to receive us into His family as a child of God.

"Behold, I stand at the door, and knock: if any man hear my voice, and open the door, I will come in to him..." (Revelation 3:20) Receiving Christ is as simple as opening the door and inviting someone in. Christ stands ready to come into your heart, forgive your sins, and make you a child of God. But he will only come by invitation. Won't you bow your head right now, wherever you are, and invite the Lord Jesus Christ to come in?

170

Lord Jesus,

I know that I am a sinner, and that I deserve to go to hell. Please forgive me and come into my heart right now. I'm trusting you to make me a child of God, to take me to Heaven when I die, and to help me live the rest of my life for you. Thank you for saving me.
In Jesus' name, Amen

If you sincerely prayed that prayer and asked the Lord to save you, He said, *"...I will come in."* That's not a maybe. He promised that He would. If you died right now with Christ in your heart where would you go? To Heaven! If you had died before you asked Christ into your heart, where would you have gone? The difference between heaven and hell is the Lord Jesus Christ living within, Who died to pay the price of our sin.

Now that Christ lives in your heart, He has promised that He will never leave. *"...for he hath said, I will never leave thee, nor forsake thee."* No matter when you die, Christ will still be in your heart as He promised, so Heaven is as sure as if you were already there.

God does expect us to obey Him after we become His children, and the very first command that He gives is found in Acts 2:38. *"...Repent, and be baptized every one of you..."* Repentance takes place within, when I turn away from sin and self and turn to Christ as my Savior. Baptism is the outward sign of what has happened in my heart --- a picture of the death, burial and resurrection of Jesus. Immediately after we get saved, God expects us to be baptized and show the world that we belong to Him.

If you have received Christ into your heart as a result of reading Revival Fires!, please write and let us know. We'd like to send you a free copy of GROWING UP IN GOD'S FAMILY and LIVING UP TO YOUR NAME.

Name
_____

Address
_____

City, State, Zip
_____

Phone Number
_____

Send to:
Dennis Corle Evangelistic Assoc. -- Revival Fires!
P.O. Box 245, Claysburg, PA 16625
(814) 239-2813